PEOPLE
IN THE NEWS

# Colin Powell

by John F. Wukovits

Lucent Books, San Diego, CA

Titles in the People in the News series include:

Garth Brooks
Jim Carrey
Bill Gates
John Grisham
Jesse Jackson
Michael Jordan
Stephen King
George Lucas
Dominique Moceanu

Rosie O'Donnell
Colin Powell
Christopher Reeve
The Rolling Stones
Steven Spielberg
R. L. Stine
Oprah Winfrey
Tiger Woods

Excerpts from *My American Journey*, by Colin L. Powell, copyright © 1995 by Colin L. Powell, are reprinted by permission of Random House, Inc.

Library of Congress Cataloging-in-Publication Data

Wukovits, John F., 1944–
    Colin Powell / by John F. Wukovits.
      p.   cm. — (People in the news)
    Includes bibliographical references and index.
    Summary: Surveys the life and military accomplishments of
  Colin Powell, as well as his struggles with racial prejudice.
    ISBN 1-56006-632-6 (lib. bdg. : alk. paper)
    1. Powell, Colin L.—Juvenile literature. 2. Generals—United States
  —Biography—Juvenile literature. 3. Afro-American generals—
  Biography—Juvenile literature. 4. United States. Army—Biography
  —Juvenile literature. [1. Powell, Colin L. 2. Generals. 3. Afro-
  Americans—Biography.] I. Title. II. People in the news
  (San Diego, Calif.)
  E840.5.P68 W85    2000
  355'.0092—dc21
  [B]                                                        99-047932

# Table of Contents

------------------------------------------

# Foreword

----------------------------------------

$F$AME AND CELEBRITY are alluring. People are drawn to those who walk in fame's spotlight, whether they are known for great accomplishments or for notorious deeds. The lives of the famous pique public interest and attract attention, perhaps because their experiences seem in some ways so different from, yet in other ways so similar to, our own.

Newspapers, magazines, and television regularly capitalize on this fascination with celebrity by running profiles of famous people. For example, television programs such as *Entertainment Tonight* devote all of their programming to stories about entertainment and entertainers. Magazines such as *People* fill their pages with stories of the private lives of famous people. Even newspapers, newsmagazines, and television news frequently delve into the lives of well-known personalities. Despite the number of articles and programs, few provide more than a superficial glimpse at their subjects.

Lucent's People in the News series offers young readers a deeper look into the lives of today's newsmakers, the influences that have shaped them, and the impact they have had in their fields of endeavor and on other people's lives. The subjects of the series hail from many disciplines and walks of life. They include authors, musicians, athletes, political leaders, entertainers, entrepreneurs, and others who have made a mark on modern life and who, in many cases, will continue to do so for years to come.

These biographies are more than factual chronicles. Each book emphasizes the contributions, accomplishments, or deeds that have brought fame or notoriety to the individual and shows how that person has influenced modern life. Authors portray their subjects in a realistic, unsentimental light. For example, Bill Gates—the cofounder and chief executive officer of the software giant Microsoft—has been instrumental in making personal computers the most vital tool of the modern age. Few dispute his business savvy, his perseverance, or his technical expertise, yet critics say he is ruthless in his dealings with competitors and driven more by his desire to maintain Microsoft's dominance in the computer industry than by an interest in furthering technology.

In these books, young readers will encounter inspiring stories about real people who achieved success despite enormous obstacles. Oprah Winfrey—the most powerful, most watched, and wealthiest woman on television today—spent the first six years of her life in the care of her grandparents while her unwed mother sought work and a better life elsewhere. Her adolescence was colored by promiscuity, pregnancy at age fourteen, rape, and sexual abuse.

Each author documents and supports his or her work with an array of primary and secondary source quotations taken from diaries, letters, speeches, and interviews. All quotes are footnoted to show readers exactly how and where biographers derive their information and provide guidance for further research. The quotations enliven the text by giving readers eyewitness views of the life and accomplishments of each person covered in the People in the News series.

In addition, each book in the series includes photographs, annotated bibliographies, timelines, and comprehensive indexes. For both the casual reader and the student researcher, the People in the News series offers insight into the lives of today's newsmakers—people who shape the way we live, work, and play in the modern age.

# Introduction

# "Dreaming About It Isn't Enough"

In April 1991 the people of New York City planned a massive parade through the downtown streets to honor the nation's newest military hero. As chairman of the Joint Chiefs of Staff during the Gulf War, four-star army general Colin L. Powell had orchestrated the country's most impressive military victory since World War II. Armed forces from the United States and other nations had attacked Saddam Hussein's Iraqi army stationed in the oil-rich Middle Eastern nation of Kuwait. With lightning speed, they smashed through Iraqi positions and sent the remnants of Hussein's forces fleeing in confusion to Iraq. The general was returning in triumph to the hometown of his youth.

## Kelly Street

By the 1940s and 1950s, Powell's Kelly Street neighborhood in the South Bronx had already begun to show the initial signs of decay. Back then, the first in what would become a wave of drug dealers appeared on corners, petty thieves were not uncommon, and abandoned buildings dotted the landscape. Though he had always set his sights on rising above his surroundings, Powell knew that for many of his classmates, Kelly Street and its immediate environs formed the boundaries of their world. For reasons varying from lack of ambition and meager parental support to prison or even violent death, most of his childhood friends and classmates never left the area.

Colin Powell left, however, not so much because he feared Kelly Street's increasing violence but because he benefited from the loving encouragement of family and friends, the example provided by an early role model, and personal determination. Rather than feeling relief that he had escaped, though, throughout his life he reflected on his formative years with fondness, for Kelly Street was home to the familiar sights, smells, and sounds of his youth and echoed with the images of past glories.

What he saw as he drove through the old neighborhood that spring morning in 1991 both encouraged and saddened him. He knew that many of the young people there would still be sucked into a life of crime and violence, but signs of renewal offered hope. The old apartment building in which he had lived had finally been demolished and replaced by a new one. Children played baseball and jumped rope in Kelly Street Park, which had been a debris-filled vacant lot only a few years earlier.

On the first stop of his victory tour of New York, Powell fulfilled a childhood dream when he tossed out the first ball at Yankee Stadium in the season opener between his hometown New York Yankees and the rival Chicago White Sox. To the

*Colin Powell (center), Secretary of Defense Dick Cheney (left), and General H. Norman Schwarzkopf attend the Gulf War victory parade in New York.*

cheers of thousands in the stands, Powell stepped to the mound and threw a strike to the waiting New York catcher.

## Inspiring Words

But the most satisfying part of his visit was speaking to the student body of his old school, Morris High. As Powell would later comment in his autobiography, not much had changed since he rushed to class in the 1950s. The building at 166th Street and Boston Road still looked more like a fort than a school. "The wooden floors still creaked, the poles for opening and closing the tall windows still hung where I remembered, and the gym, where I was to speak, had the familiar smell of sweat and disinfectant."[1]

Students and faculty erupted into applause as Powell strode to the podium. Once the cheering subsided, Powell gazed at the audience for a moment before uttering his first words. Little had changed among the student body, either, as mainly black and Hispanic youth stared back at him. Powell knew what he wanted to convey, for it was a message that he not only delivered to youth groups wherever he traveled, but more importantly, it was a message that he had lived his entire life.

*Powell speaks to the students at a junior high school. While in New York in 1991, Powell revisited his old high school, Morris High, to give a similar speech.*

"I remember this place," he said of his old school. "I remember the feeling that you can't make it." Powell emphasized the next words, for they were the ones he most wanted the teenagers to recall. "But you can. When I was coming up, the opportunities were limited. But now they are there. You can be anything you want to be."

Powell then admonished the student body that simply wanting something is only part of the battle, that many people form dreams but do not realize them. "But wanting to be isn't enough. Dreaming about it isn't enough. You've got to study for it, work for it, fight for it with all your heart and soul."

He urged the students to select good role models, whether they happened to be "black or white, a general or a teacher, or just the parents who brought you into the world."[2] Powell had chosen to join the army because of such a role model, and he knew how important such a person could be for the current generation of students.

Powell told the crowd that 97 percent of the soldiers currently in the army had graduated from high school, and their success stood as a shining example for the students at Morris High School to resist the temptation to drop out of school. A diploma, according to Powell, was proof that the person

> will stick to the task given. Somebody who, growing in their life at age fourteen, fifteen, sixteen, seventeen, when faced with a challenge of hard work, of study, of commitment, of responsibility . . . met the challenge, stayed in high school, and got the diploma. It shows that you can overcome obstacles. If you don't get that high school diploma, you're on your way to nowhere. You're on your way to the dead end.[3]

## "A Path That Leads Somewhere"

Powell wrote later, "I do not know if I reached a single youngster that day. But I was determined to leave Morris High with a message for those kids. Reject the easy path of victimhood. Dare to take the harder path of work and commitment, a path that leads somewhere."[4]

## Army Officer Ranks

In his career, Colin Powell rose to the top levels of the army. Few ever reach four-star or five-star rank, so Powell stands in excellent company. The ranks are as follows, from lowest to highest:

- second lieutenant
- first lieutenant
- captain
- major
- lieutenant colonel
- colonel
- brigadier general—one star
- major general—two stars
- lieutenant general—three stars
- general—four stars (Powell's highest rank)
- general of the army—five stars (only a handful have attained this rank, such as Dwight D. Eisenhower in World War II)

He could have pointed to his own career as a model of how to succeed. From his origins in a racially diverse New York neighborhood, Powell moved to a world inhabited by presidents, kings, generals, and leaders. He advanced from a college Reserve Officers' Training Corps (ROTC) to the nation's top military post. He grew up when bigotry and discrimination pushed African Americans to the background, but he succeeded through sheer determination and hard work. He began his military career by commanding a few hundred soldiers in Europe and ended it thirty-five years later with more than 2 million soldiers, sailors, airmen, and marines under his command.

Powell's story, which took him to all corners of the globe and brought him world fame and adulation, began in the streets of New York City, where a loving mother and father gently but firmly prodded their son to make something of himself.

- - - - - - - - - - - - - - - - - - - - - - - - - - - - - - - - - - - - -

# Chapter 1

# "A Neat Place to Grow Up"

BORN APRIL 5, 1937, the son of Jamaican immigrants, Colin Luther Powell joined a family built on a foundation of love and hard work.

Like many black Americans, slavery is a part of Colin Powell's family history. The island of Jamaica, where the Powell family history begins, was part of the British Empire for nearly three hundred years, and many native Jamaicans therefore labored under British rule. In the 1800s, Powell's maternal grandfather served as the overseer of a Jamaican sugar plantation. Other relatives tilled the land as peasant farmers, and his grandmother's family worked as slaves. However, slavery in Jamaica had little in common with the slavery that flourished in the United States. In Jamaica, slaves were treated more like hired workers than servants. They could own a plot of land and farm it for profit, and few limitations restricted their opportunities to improve their situation. As James Watson, one of Powell's cousins explains, "As a result, we don't say, 'I can't.' We say, 'I'll try.'"[5]

## Strong Parents

Powell's parents, Luther and Maud, immigrated to the United States during the great influx of Jamaicans shortly after the turn of the twentieth century. In the early 1900s thousands of Jamaicans, eager to improve their lives, headed to the Harlem area of New York City. Among them were Luther Theophilus Powell and Maud Ariel McKoy. The two initially met at a picnic, and they were later married in Harlem on December 28,

11

1929. Six years after the birth of daughter Marilyn, Colin joined the family.

Though short at five feet four inches, Luther Powell stood in no man's shadow. The quiet man preferred to let actions speak for him. Hard work in New York's garment district carried him from the warehouse to the post of foreman. The elder Powell was both kind and compassionate. He was very active in the Episcopal Church, and he frequently brought home clothes or fabric from work to give to needy individuals. Still others sought his advice or help in landing a job.

Luther Powell's enthusiasm was shared by his entire family. His son later wrote that

> Luther Powell never let his race or station affect his sense of self. West Indians like him had come to this country with nothing. Every morning they got on that subway, worked like dogs all day, got home at 8:00 at night, supported their families, and educated their children. If they could do that, how dare anyone think they were less than anybody's equal? That was Pop's attitude.[6]

Like her husband, Maud Powell was a hard worker and an enthusiastic wife and mother. She worked long hours as a seamstress in the garment district, then came home to take care of the children and house, still fresh with vitality. "When I picture Mom, she is always wearing an apron, bustling around our apartment, always in motion, cooking, washing, ironing, sewing, after working all day downtown in the garment district as a seamstress sewing buttons and trim on clothing."[7]

Maud proudly proclaimed her fidelity to the local garment union and made a point of teasing her husband, who, as a foreman, was part of management. She also reveled in the fact that while she had earned her high school diploma, her husband had not. Whenever they verbally sparred, Maud loved to hold her achievement over Luther's head.

## A New Neighborhood

When Colin was three years old, the family moved from Harlem to the Hunt's Point section of the South Bronx. Luther and Maud had seen signs of rapid decay in Harlem and believed that the family would be much safer in the new neighborhood. There, the family lived in a four-bedroom apartment for three years before moving into their own four-bedroom flat on Kelly Street.

Still, Hunt's Point was no quiet suburban plot with white picket fences, manicured lawns, and pretty homes. Families locked their doors and fastened windows to prevent the burglaries that had become too common. A drug trade, although not as flourishing as it would become in later years, had begun to emerge. Street fights and knifings marked the arrival of gangs battling for their turf.

And yet, according to Colin Powell, Hunt's Point offered stability. He never felt that he belonged to a "minority" group because everyone on Kelly Street was a minority. Blacks, Puerto Ricans, Jews, and Eastern Europeans lived together in harmony, which produced tolerance and friendliness among most residents.

More importantly, families remained intact. Even though Luther and Maud put long hours into their jobs, the children

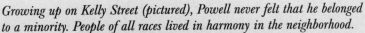
*Growing up on Kelly Street (pictured), Powell never felt that he belonged to a minority. People of all races lived in harmony in the neighborhood.*

never felt abandoned. Neighbors and relatives who lived nearby watched the children. As Powell's sister, Marilyn, later explained, "We were always closely supervised." She added, "When you walked down the street, you had all these eyes watching you."[8]

When an eight-year-old Colin skipped school one day, a family friend spotted him sneaking back home. In response, his parents arranged for a relative or friend to take their son by the hand and personally deliver him each morning to the school door.

Besides knowing that family and neighbors watched out for him, what made Powell describe Kelly Street as "a neat place to grow up"[9] were the friends with whom he enjoyed his childhood. He and his cohorts spent their Saturdays at the neighborhood theater, the Tiffany, watching movies, a string of serial adventures, and cartoons. "With your grubby little hand clutching a dirty quarter," he told an interviewer, "and with whatever food was necessary to last you for the rest of the day, you went to the Tiffany, and watched cowboy movie after cowboy movie, and threw things at each other, and generally misbehaved, I expect."[10]

In nearby parks, Powell and his buddies played war games with toy soldiers and model airplanes. Like most young boys who grew up in the immediate aftermath of World War II and while the Korean War was being fought, warfare was a large part of Powell's youth. Military figures commanded respect and their crisp uniforms, glistening with medals, drew admiration. Powell and his friends lost themselves in mock battles and glorious triumphs. "Warfare held a certain fascination for me, as it often does for boys who have not yet seen it up close."[11]

## A Mediocre Student

Colin attended New York's public schools, but the quiet boy was not a star student. As he moved into the fourth grade, for instance, his teacher placed him in the lowest reading group, which had been set aside for those considered slow in learning.

Colin did not lack academic skill, he just had not yet discovered something that stirred his passion. His parents stressed the value of a good education and told their children that a college degree was essential, but their son seemed uninterested in his studies.

## "Free All!"

Like most children, Powell enjoyed playing outside with his friends. He became famous in his neighborhood for one game called ring-a-levio, as friend Tony Grant explains in Howard Means's book *Colin Powell*.

You chose up sides, maybe four to six on a side. One side ran, and the other side chased. When you caught someone, you put them in a den, an enclosed area of some kind. You could free the people who had been caught on your side by breaking into the den and yelling, "Free all!" Guys had different ways of trying to break in. Some would be sneaky about it; some would try to negotiate for one or two people. Colin, if he saw someone had been caught, would come flying in with his body from half a block away and free them all.

He tried playing the piano, but he gave it up. He turned to the flute, but that, too, drifted by the wayside. While his sister, Marilyn, studied long hours to achieve superb grades, Colin was just happy to pass his classes. He lacked focus in any area.

Powell emerged from his shell during his junior high years. He was named class captain at the all-male New York public school, showing that his fellow students admired him, and he worked at a string of jobs after school. However, his report cards still showed the same mediocre grades.

## High-School Friends and Lessons

Powell's parents hoped that their son could enter New York's prestigious Stuyvesant High School, but his lackadaisical performance throughout elementary and junior high school doomed his chances. Instead, he entered Morris High School in September 1950.

As in junior high, Powell was popular among his classmates but was hardly held in esteem by his teachers or coaches. Powell tried out for the cross-country team, but he quit after realizing how difficult it was to run long distances. Thinking he could handle short sprints, he joined the track team but soon dropped it as well. He even left the church basketball squad after sitting on the bench for a few games. Powell's habit of quitting worried his parents, who hoped that Colin would quickly stumble across something that ignited his interest.

## Family Expectations

Powell learned what was expected of him not only from his parents'
words but also, and perhaps more importantly, from their actions. In
the following excerpt from the 1992 cumulation *Biography Today*
magazine, author Laurie Harris explains that Luther and Maud Powell
exemplified how hard work and dedication could pay dividends.

He [Colin Powell] and Marilyn and their many cousins were
raised in an atmosphere of hard work and solid expectations.
Demonstrating a willingness to work and to sacrifice was the
parents' way of setting an example for the children. Powell, re-
calling those days, told an interviewer how they all got together
on weekends and "somehow, over time, they made it clear to us
that there were certain expectations built into the family system. It was unthinkable not to be educated, get a job, go as far
as you could, whether it meant becoming Chairman of the Joint
Chiefs or having a good job as a nurse."

His parents were encouraged by his extracurricular activities. Colin was such a good employee at Sickser's Furniture Store
that the owner promoted him from stock boy to salesman. His
love of tradition and discipline at church led him to serve as a
top altar boy at St. Margaret's Episcopal Church. He seemed to
make good choices in friends, especially Gene Norman, a fellow
West Indian, and Tony Grant.

One summer Colin had attended a church camp and associ-
ated with a rough group of teens. The boys sneaked out of camp,
purchased some beer, and hid it in the toilet tank to keep it cool.
Unfortunately for the boys, the camp priest uncovered the supply of alcohol. When he gathered everyone to ask who was responsible, only Powell rose to admit his part in the incident.
Eventually the other boys confessed, and the entire group was
placed on a train and sent back home.

Knowing that his parents would already have been contacted with the news, Colin "dragged myself up Winchester
Avenue and turned right onto Kelly Street like a felon mounting
the gallows." Both parents were ready to hand out a severe punishment to their remorseful son when the camp priest called.
While Colin had done wrong, the priest explained that he

should be commended for taking responsibility for his actions like an adult. "From a juvenile delinquent, I had been catapulted to hero. Something from that boyhood experience, the rewards of honesty, hit home and stayed."[12]

The fact that he was black did not appear to make a significant impact on Powell during these years. His parents emphasized that hard work led to success, and the wondrous mixture of minorities in his Kelly Street neighborhood reinforced the notion that everyone was equal. In 1953 his sister, Marilyn, married a white man, Norman Berns. While Luther Powell initially worried about the problems his daughter would encounter in an interracial marriage, Marilyn and Norman Berns have enjoyed a long union. In 1999 they celebrated their forty-seventh anniversary.

During Powell's high-school years, Kelly Street was changing for the worse. Drug dealers could be found on the street corner trying to sell heroin, and violent crimes were occurring more frequently. Though the lure of quick profit from the drug trade attracted many young people, Powell never touched drugs. The love he had for and from his family, along with the sense of right that his parents instilled, kept him from drugs. As Powell recalls,

My parents would have killed me, but the second reason is that . . . it was stupid. It was the most self-destructive thing you could do with the life God and your parents had given to you. . . . Of all the kids that I grew up with on Kelly Street, Gene Norman and one or two others made it. Too many of the others did not make it. They went to jail, or they died, or they were never heard from again."[13]

*Detectives investigate a murder on Kelly Street. The neighborhood changed for the worse during Powell's years in high school.*

## Main Intellectual Influences

Colin Powell feels strongly about the importance of role models in people's lives. As a young man he started learning about the great personalities of American history, and three of these historical figures have particularly influenced him: Thomas Jefferson, Abraham Lincoln, and Martin Luther King Jr.

Powell loves reading the works of founding father Thomas Jefferson. He appreciates Jefferson's belief in the goodness of people and that good will triumph over evil in a democracy. Likewise, he reveres President Abraham Lincoln for extending freedom to slaves, creating black military units, and for not letting the severe differences between the North and the South prevent him from doing what he felt was correct. Finally, Powell admires civil rights leader Martin Luther King Jr., who he claims finished the work begun by Lincoln. As he mentioned in David Roth's biography, *Sacred Honor*, "Lincoln freed the slaves, but Martin Luther King set the rest of the nation free."

*Thomas Jefferson.*

## College Years

Though Powell had wallowed academically in the middle of his high-school class, he passed enough courses to graduate in three and a half years with a C average. One of the notions taken for granted in the Powell family was that the young men and women attend college. The older generation wanted their children to enjoy a better life than they had, and they believed that college was essential to this wish. Powell had no great desire to rush into higher education, but family tradition dictated college, so he applied to City College of New York (CCNY), which catered to students from New York neighborhoods, and New York University (NYU). When both institutions accepted him,

Powell chose CCNY because it cost only $10 a year while NYU wanted $750.

Powell did not know what he wanted to be when he started college. His mother suggested the engineering program because of the financial rewards offered by that occupation, and Powell, having no other idea in mind, followed her advice. Though he achieved B's in his classwork, engineering bored him. He remembers listening to a lecture on mechanical drawing. "A professor said to me, 'Imagine a plane intersecting a cone in space.' I said, 'I cannot imagine a plane intersecting a cone in space. I'm out of here.'"[14] Powell switched his major to geology because that subject interested him more than the others.

Like most college students, Powell worked during summer break to help pay for textbooks and other necessary items. That first summer he worked with other college-age men at the local Pepsi-Cola bottling plant. While his white peers worked the machines, however, he was given a mop and told to clean the floors. Rather than being offended at what some would consider a racial slight or complain about the unfairness, Powell decided to do the best he could. "I took the mop. If that was what I had

*An ROTC color guard stands at attention during a parade. The orderliness and organization of the ROTC appealed to Powell while he was at CCNY.*

to do to earn $65 a week, I'd do it. I'd mop the place until it glowed in the dark."[15] He performed his job so well that the foreman told him he had earned a spot on the machinery the next summer.

Though Powell had shown flashes of ingenuity and hard work, he had no idea what he hoped to do with his life. However, his uncertainty dissolved one day as he walked along the CCNY campus and spotted a group of uniformed students marching in precise formation. Powell liked their orderliness and organization, and he felt a quick rapport with the students, who were part of the campus ROTC contingent. This chance meeting would lead Colin Powell into the military and to future acclaim.

------------------------------------------------

# Chapter 2

# "A Sense of Belonging"

Powell JOINED THE ROTC in the fall of 1954, signing on for the Pershing Rifles, an elite precision drill team and honor guard. Since the Pershing Rifles demanded more time and discipline from its members than other ROTC teams, those who joined usually intended to make the army a career rather than a step toward something else. They practiced for hours after classes to be the best.

## Powell Finds a Home

With fifteen hundred cadets, CCNY hosted the largest ROTC group in the nation. Powell loved its structure and sense of family. "At this point, not a single Kelly Street friend of mine was going to college. I was seventeen. I felt cut off and lonely. The uniform gave me a sense of belonging, and something I had never experienced all the while I was growing up; I felt distinctive." [16]

Powell and the other Pershing Rifles formed a tight-knit group that studied together, marched together, and chased girls together. They took pride in the blue-and-white shoulder cords and enamel crests on their uniforms that distinguished the group from other ROTC members. As Powell recalls,

> The PRs [Pershing Rifles] would go to the limit for each other and for the group. If this was what soldiering was all about, then maybe I wanted to be a soldier. . . . The discipline, the structure, the camaraderie, the sense of belonging were what I craved. I became a leader almost immediately. [17]

Powell's first role model outside of his family was ROTC cadet colonel Ronnie Brooks. Brooks issued orders with decisiveness and made decisions quickly. Powell respected Brooks's natural ability to command, and Powell concluded that the cadet colonel had all the qualities that he then lacked, particularly organization, decision-making skills, and clear goals. Powell decided that he would try to follow in Brooks's footsteps.

## ROTC Leadership

Though Powell still earned average grades in other subjects, he excelled in every military history and ROTC class. He took the drilling more seriously than his Pershing Rifles counterparts, and he exhibited the ability to lead others. By his senior year, Powell had succeeded the departed Brooks as cadet colonel and had set his sights on a long career with the army.

As good a cadet colonel as Powell was, he still had much to learn about leadership. The Pershing Rifles sponsored two drill teams, the regular squad and a special trick drill team. Both entered competitions against other ROTC teams. In his junior year, Powell had guided the trick team to an impressive victory, but because of his new duties, he relinquished control in his senior year to another cadet, John Pardo. Instead, Powell took over the regular drill team.

Powell wanted both teams to capture first place in that year's competition. However, he noticed that Pardo lacked the necessary enthusiasm and focus that the trick drill team needed. When he learned from other members that Pardo and his girlfriend were in the midst of a dispute, Powell considered taking over the squad himself. He relented when Pardo assured him that he could cast aside his personal problems and lead the team to a championship.

In the end, Powell's regular drill team won its division, but Pardo's lost. Even worse, Pardo's failure meant that the Pershing Rifles finished second in the overall competition, a huge disappointment to Powell. He felt that he had betrayed the Pershing Rifles by not removing Pardo, but he also felt that he had failed Pardo by allowing him to remain in his post without adequate preparation. Powell wrote later,

That day I started absorbing a lesson as valid for a cadet in a musty college drill hall as for a four-star general in the Pentagon. I learned that being in charge means making decisions, no matter how unpleasant. If it's broke, fix it. When you do, you win the gratitude of the people who have been suffering under the bad situation. I learned in a college drill competition that you cannot let the mission suffer, or make the majority pay to spare the feelings of an individual.[18]

To remind himself of this incident while he was a general in Washington, D.C., Powell kept a note under the glass on his desk saying that being responsible meant you sometimes had to upset people.

## Summer ROTC

ROTC cadets were required to spend a summer at a military camp to learn the basics of military life. In the summer of 1957 Luther Powell drove his son and two ROTC friends to a bus station where they would board a bus for their required camp stay at Fort Bragg, North Carolina. The elder Powell was anxious about the plans. This was the first time that his son would travel into the South, where racism was rampant, and he was concerned for his son's safety.

The segregated South of the time subjected blacks to repeated indignities. There, blacks lived in the poorer sections of town. Blacks had to use separate rest rooms, drink from separate fountains, and attend separate schools—not because they wanted to but because it was public policy. Luther Powell knew that it took little for a black man to incite the rage of whites, and he wondered if he would ever see his son again.

Luther need not have worried, for his son barely interacted with southern society. As soon as the bus arrived, an army vehicle whisked the cadets to Fort Bragg, where Powell spent six weeks in training. He never once set foot in town. However, he did notice the signs designating water fountains and rest rooms as "Colored" or "White" and that black officers at Fort Bragg had to use a different officers' club than their white counterparts.

*A black man climbs the stairs to the colored entrance of a theater in the South. Powell's first experience with segregation was at ROTC camp in North Carolina.*

In spite of this, Powell reveled in every aspect of training. He loved handling weapons and learning how to camouflage a position, and he registered outstanding marks in every activity. His enthusiasm gained him the honors for "Best Cadet, Company D" and placed him second for the entire camp.

The night before returning home, a white supply sergeant asked Powell if he knew why he had not been named best cadet in camp. When Powell replied that he had not given the matter any thought, the sergeant explained, "You think these Southern ROTC instructors are going to go back to their colleges and say the best kid here was a Negro?" [19] Powell was stunned at the realization that his skin color had been used to negatively judge him.

## Graduation

On June 9, 1958, Powell was sworn into the U.S. Army. Because he had performed so well in his military classes and at his duties as cadet colonel, Powell was offered a regular, rather than reserve, commission. In other words, while most of his friends from ROTC would spend two years in the army, Powell was asked to remain for three. He happily accepted the offer.

That night Powell and his friends celebrated their commissions at a series of area bars, continuing their festivities well into the next morning even though CCNY's commencement ceremonies were scheduled for that day. Powell had posted an unspectacular series of C's in his geology classes at City College, and the degree he had earned seemed to him almost incidental to his ROTC work. Why bother with graduation, he wondered, when one could enjoy a few moments with friends?

Powell's mother, who impatiently waited in the college's auditorium for her absent son, felt differently. According to Powell, "She knew where I was and sent some friends over to ask me if I'd be kind enough to join the graduation ceremonies."[20] Somewhat chastised, he left the bar and joined his family.

*Soldiers learn how to use a bazooka. At Fort Bragg, Powell excelled in weapons handling and other military activities.*

## Training Camp

Armed with a college diploma and an army commission, Second Lieutenant Colin Powell headed to Fort Benning, Georgia, for five months of training. He started out by mastering the fundamentals of commanding men in frontline combat in the Infantry Officer Basic Course. He learned how to move small units about a battlefield, how to position a rifle squad, how to establish a sound defensive perimeter, and how to handle prisoners of war. Survival-and-evasion tactics and hand-to-hand combat lessons reminded the soldiers of the brutality of warfare, and a string of obstacle courses challenged their physical fitness.

The other soldiers were impressed with Powell's obvious leadership skills. William Roosma, who completed the same training course, commented about Powell, "One of the things that struck you was his maturity, even at a very young age. He had a sense of confidence about himself that was like an aura."[21]

Following his basic training, in which he was ranked among the top ten candidates for best trainee, Powell moved on to two months of intensive ranger training. As one of the elite military units, comparable to the navy SEALs, the U.S. Army Rangers take pride in being tough, efficient, and superb fighters. Consequently, their training is considered the army's most demanding. Carrying a full field pack weighing fifty pounds, Powell miserably sloshed day and night through swamps, where he and the other trainees lived off of rattlesnake and alligator meat. The rangers conducted mountain operations in which Powell had to scale cliffs, ford streams, and slide across ropes traversing ravines. One nighttime activity called for Powell's group to locate a stake stuck in the ground using only a compass for navigation.

*An Army Ranger crosses a makeshift bridge.*

## Why Would You Fight?

Some wonder why a black in the 1950s, who suffered the stings of segregation and saw society slam doors of opportunity in his face, would want to serve in the military. If the nation does not accord true equality, why be willing to die for it? Powell tried to answer that question in his autobiography, *My American Journey.*

> Why have blacks, nevertheless, always answered the nation's call? They have done so to exercise their rights as citizens in the one area where it was permitted. They did it because they believed that if they demonstrated equal courage and equal sacrifice in fighting and dying for their country, then equality of opportunity surely must follow.

"I can remember the moment I had my first doubt about the career I had chosen," stated Powell. "It happened in the mountains of northern Georgia as I hurried along a cable at a height of one hundred feet, seconds from being smashed against a large tree. This exercise was called the Slide for Life, and the Army was making me perform it to see if I was scared. I was." [22]

The Slide for Life was designed to test whether the trainees would obey orders that seemed almost suicidal. In the heat of battle, soldiers must instantly obey, and this exercise was a stringent test of their willingness to follow orders. Instructors had strung a cable across a river, steeply sloping toward a clump of trees on the other side. One by one, trainees grabbed hold of the cable and descended at what seemed lightning speed, hoping that the instructor across the river yelled "Drop!" before they smashed into the trees. For one horrifying moment Powell was sure he was about to die, but just then the instructor ordered him to drop, and Powell happily plunged to the water below.

Powell again second guessed his career choice while learning to parachute in airborne school. While standing in an aircraft moments before jumping into the void outside, Powell doubted his sanity. Fear enveloped the young soldier, but he gathered enough courage to fling himself away from the plane and trust in his parachute.

Powell needed to show courage away from the obstacle courses as well. Though the military had been desegregated in

1948 by President Harry S. Truman, Powell still experienced racism whenever he left Fort Benning and headed into a nearby town. On occasion his white friends tried to force town bartenders to serve Powell, but he often had to swallow his anger and tell his buddies to go into town without him. Powell and other blacks could shop at local department stores, but they were not allowed to eat at the stores' lunch counters. Powell could walk along city streets, but he risked confrontation if he even looked at a white woman. The sad reality that he could wear the uniform of the U.S. Army—even die in the nation's defense—yet could not enjoy equal citizenship with white southerners, galled Powell.

Instead of acting out in anger, Powell internalized his feelings. "If people in the South insisted on living by crazy rules, then I would play the hand dealt me for now. If I was to be confined to one end of the playing field, then I was going to be a star on that part of the field." He added that while Southern injustice repulsed him, "most of all I felt challenged. I'll show you!"[23]

## On to West Germany

In January 1959 Powell was sent to West Germany to command a platoon of forty men. Their duty was to help guard the Fulda Gap, one of the likely avenues of advancement into Europe should the Soviet army begin hostilities on that continent. Stationed less than fifty miles from the Communist-controlled East German border, Powell found himself in one of the world's potential hot spots.

Powell performed his command there smoothly. He treated his men fairly yet demanded that they always strive for excellence. A July 1959 efficiency report praised Powell's ability to deal with those above and below him and concluded that he had a promising future in the military. Consequently, Powell was promoted to first lieutenant on December 29, 1959.

In Germany, Powell learned that most soldiers, although they may not admit it, want to be pushed to their limits. He frequently heard the men complain about his constant drills and lengthy runs but then wonder afterward if they had bettered their prior results. A good performance boosted morale, and

## A Singer in Germany

One of Colin Powell's more pleasant surprises during his time in West Germany occurred along a narrow side road. In the midst of conducting maneuvers with his troops, they came upon a jeep from another unit. Some of his men walked over to the jeep, then shouted to Powell to come over to take a look. Powell related the incident in his autobiography, *My American Journey*.

> I walked over to the jeep, where a grimy, weary-looking sergeant saluted me and put out his hand. It was Elvis Presley. . . . What impressed me at the time was that instead of seeking celebrity treatment, Elvis had done his two-year hitch, uncomplainingly, as an ordinary GI, even rising to the responsibility of an NCO (Non-Commissioned Officer).

*While stationed in West Germany, Powell met Sergeant Elvis Presley (pictured).*

Powell grasped that this was one way to build an efficient platoon. Americans love to win, he concluded, and they respect someone who demands the best.

Powell also gained a healthy respect for death in West Germany when an errant artillery shell from the base's practice range exploded near the soldiers' quarters. It was early 1960 and Powell had just picked up a tray of food when he heard an ominous whistling sound and, moments later, a terrific explosion shook the area. "I dropped the food and rushed toward the blast as dismembered legs, hands, and arms thumped to the ground around me. . . . I had seen a hundred war movies, but nothing had prepared me for the sights I saw that day."[24] Powell had just witnessed death at close hand, a sight to which he would have to become accustomed throughout his career.

## A Return to the United States

After successfully fulfilling his duties in West Germany, in January 1961 Powell took the lessons he learned in Europe to Fort Devens, Massachusetts, for his next assignment. There, Powell received command of a company even though the post normally went to a captain rather than a first lieutenant. He soon engaged his company in a series of competitions. Instead of confining the contests to the athletic fields, Powell widened the focus. Men vied for best barracks, best weapons inspections, best anything. Powell wanted his men to gain self-esteem, and he believed that these competitions helped instill confidence.

In the summer of 1961 Powell completed his three years service. Though he could have left the army at that time, the thought never crossed his mind. He loved what he was doing, and he could think of few areas in American society where a black man could achieve success as fairly as in the army. American society at large still stacked the cards against blacks, but the army did its best to ensure fair play. He later wrote that

> less discrimination, a truer merit system, and leveler playing fields existed inside the gates of our military posts than in any Southern city hall or Northern corporation. The Army, therefore, made it easier for me to love my country, with all its flaws, and to serve her with all my heart.[25]

## Love and Marriage

His heart, as he would soon learn, would open to more than just the military. While Powell had enjoyed dating in high school and college, no one girl had attracted serious interest. That changed shortly before Thanksgiving 1961 when he went on a blind date with Alma Johnson.

Powell was stricken by Johnson's beauty and charm. "She was fair-skinned, with light brown hair and a lovely figure. I was mesmerized by a pair of luminous eyes, an unusual shade of green. Miss Johnson moved gracefully and spoke graciously, with a soft Southern accent."[26]

For her part, when her friend mentioned the possibility of going out with a soldier, Johnson answered that she did not like blind dates and had no intention of becoming involved with a soldier. Her friend, however, persisted and a reluctant Johnson finally gave in.

Her first sight of Powell hardy reassured the dubious female. "He looked like he was about twelve years old." Johnson wondered to herself, "All right, who is this baby?"[27]

But Johnson warmed to her companion the longer that they talked. They enjoyed a meal and a visit to a nightclub for dancing and more talk, including a chat about Powell's career plans. Johnson asked how long Powell intended to stay in the military and was surprised that he wanted to remain in the army for his

*After some hesitation, Alma Johnson (seen here with her husband in 1989 as he is sworn into office as Chairman of the Joint Chiefs of Staff) agreed to go on a blind date with Powell.*

entire career. Every soldier she had met was eager to leave as soon as possible, but Powell loved his occupation. She was not sure whether this man was crazy or ambitious.

Powell called the next day to ask Johnson for another date. She accepted, and before long she was making weekend treks to Fort Devens to be with Powell. Like her future husband, Alma Johnson warmed to the friendliness and comaraderie shown by those in the army. "It's a sense of community and belonging. Military people reach out to people very easily because of the very transient nature [of being in the service]. You make friends and you welcome new ones, and I liked that very much." [28]

In August 1962, just a little more than six months after their first date, Powell received orders to join a small contingent of American officers serving in Vietnam as military advisers to the South Vietnamese army. Though the conflict between that army and rival Communist forces had not yet exploded into the full-scale war it would become later in the decade, Powell was headed to a war zone where serious injury and even death was a possibility.

An American officer conducts bayonet practice with a South Vietnamese soldier. Beginning in 1962, Powell served as a military adviser to the South Vietnamese army.

When he told Johnson of his assignment, she replied that she could not wait for a man who may or may not want her when he returned from overseas duty. Was he serious about her, she wanted to know, or should she consider the relationship over? Powell lay awake all night pondering the issue, then drove back the next day and proposed marriage in an awkward sort of way.

"Okay," he said to Johnson, "this is what we are going to do. We'll get married in two weeks. You'll go home next week to get ready for the wedding, I'll come down the week after that, and we'll get married." [29]

The wedding took place in Johnson's hometown of Birmingham, Alabama, a town then considered one of the most racist in the nation. At first Luther and Maud Powell hesitated to go, explaining that they feared traveling into the Deep South. When they learned that Colin's sister, Marilyn, and her husband, Norm, had made arrangements to attend the wedding, they changed their minds, figuring with dark humor that "if they lynch Norm [for being with a black female] we all ought to be there." [30]

With fellow Pershing Rifle Ronnie Brooks as best man and Johnson's sister Barbara as maid of honor, Colin and Alma married on August 25, 1962. They had precious few weeks to enjoy their marriage, however, because within four months Colin Powell would be in the steamy jungles of Vietnam.

# Chapter 3

----------------------------------------

# "Half-Hearted Warfare"

**W**HILE MOST PEOPLE would shy away from entering a dangerous area, career military officers proudly accept the assignment to a war zone, for leadership in combat is the reason they joined the service. Colin Powell, too, proudly accepted the assignment to Vietnam, where he learned valuable lessons in combat and leadership that he would remember years later.

## Preparation for Battle

Vietnam is located along the South China Sea in Southeast Asia. Since 1954 the nation had been divided into two sections—a Communist-controlled North Vietnam and a supposedly democratic South Vietnam. Many inhabitants in the south hated the repressive policies of their government, however, and were openly sympathetic to the Communists. They formed their own army, the Vietcong, and waged a guerrilla war with the South Vietnamese government.

To counter the Communist threat, the United States sent military advisers to help build an efficient, powerful South Vietnamese army. Powell's selection as an adviser was an honor for the young soldier, as only the most promising officers received the assignment.

Before departing for Vietnam, Powell first had to attend a training course back at Fort Bragg, North Carolina, where, despite the honor of his position, he and his wife had to endure racism. As Colin and Alma Powell drove from Alabama to North Carolina, for example, they often could not even locate a gas station that

*American soldiers charge through a rice paddy in Vietnam. At first, the U.S. sent military advisers to South Vietnam to counter the Communist threat.*

allowed them to use its rest rooms. Instead, the Powells had to pull off to the side of the road to relieve themselves.

Once they arrived in North Carolina, Colin Powell had trouble finding housing. Dispirited, he was about to send Alma back to her parents in Birmingham when an officer he knew from Germany, Joe Schwar, insisted that the couple live with him and his family. Whites courted danger in the South at that time by welcoming a black couple into their home, but the Schwars were not about to let the Powells be separated. Colin Powell wrote later that "what the Schwars did for two desperate newlyweds long years ago is one of the great kindnesses that Alma and I have ever experienced."[31]

Powell completed the training course without mishap and was promoted to captain. After saying goodbye to the Schwars, he drove Alma, who was now pregnant, to Birmingham, where she would live while he served his tour of duty overseas. On Christmas morning 1962, just four months after their wedding, Powell arrived in Vietnam.

## The Camp at A Shau Valley

Powell's station stood in the remote A Shau Valley, the home of four hundred South Vietnamese troops. The post near the Laotian border was established to cut the flow of men and material pouring into the nation in support of the Communists. The supply route, a series of jungle paths called the Ho Chi Minh Trail, brought men, food, and ammunition from North Vietnam, through Laos, and into South Vietnam.

Powell served as adviser to Captain Vo Cong Hieu, the commander of the Second Battalion, Third Regiment, First Infantry Division. Powell's task was to build leadership, unity, and a sense of purpose in the Vietnamese soldiers and to accompany them on patrols aimed at severing the flow of supplies.

Powell's first look at the camp in the remote A Shau Valley rattled him:

> I felt as if I had been propelled backward in time. Shimmering in the heat of the sun was an earth-and-

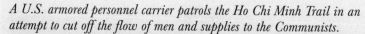

*A U.S. armored personnel carrier patrols the Ho Chi Minh Trail in an attempt to cut off the flow of men and supplies to the Communists.*

wood fortress ringed by pillboxes [sheltered gun posi-
tions]. . . . I stood there asking myself the question I am
sure Roman legionnaires must have asked in Gaul—
what the hell am I doing here?[32]

More dismaying than the camp itself was a prevailing sense
of insanity about the endeavor. When Powell asked Hieu why
the base had been placed in a valley—where the enemy could
easily lob shells from camouflaged positions on the surrounding
mountains—the Vietnamese commander replied that the camp
was established to protect the rough airstrip hacked out of the
jungle. When Powell asked why the airfield existed, Hieu said it
was there to supply the base.

Hieu's illogical answer—that the base existed to protect an
airfield that was built to supply the base—stunned Powell. It
would not, however, be the last time in Vietnam that Powell felt
such frustration. "I would spend nearly twenty years, one way or
another, grappling with our experience in this country. And
over all that time, Vietnam rarely made much more sense than
Captain Hieu's circular reasoning on the January day in 1963."[33]

## Jungle Patrols

Powell had grown up with a staple of World War II stories and
movies, but he found a different type of war in Southeast Asia,
where frontal attacks were the exception. Rather, hit-and-run as-
saults from an elusive enemy dominated. Besides the marine helicopter pilot who brought in food and mail, Powell never saw
another American. He saw the enemy even less.

Jungle patrols frequently lasted for weeks, although they
rarely located the enemy. Instead, soldiers battled with the vines,
towering trees and branches, muggy climate, and huge leeches
that mysteriously wormed their way through layers of clothing,
sunk their teeth into a soldier's skin, and sucked out his blood.

Daily Vietcong ambushes frustrated the ranks. Still, Powell
noticed that the men on point—the squad that walked ahead of
the rest of the column—were not wearing the protective vests
made from crisscrossed layers of woven nylon. Hieu saw no purpose in them, but Powell argued that the vests could save lives.

Powell's insistence paid dividends one day when a soldier on point survived a bullet that smacked into his vest. Powell pried out the flattened bullet and showed it to the other South Vietnamese soldiers, whose reluctance to wear the vests quickly disappeared.

The vests could not, however, protect everyone, and Powell's first experience with death in combat was as profound as it was sudden. As he plodded through the jungle, Powell heard shouts and screams. The Vietcong had attacked, fired a few quick rounds, then melted into the foliage. He hustled to the front to find several wounded soldiers and one dead. Though he knew the violent nature of warfare, he had never seen death in such close proximity before. "The exhilaration of a cocky twenty-five-year-old American had evaporated in a single burst of gunfire." [34]

Not long after, Powell himself almost became a casualty when an enemy shell exploded directly above him. Fortunately, Powell stood beneath the thick branches of a large tree, which sheltered him from the bits of lethal metal fragments that whistled by right and left. Powell earned high marks for his work with the South Vietnamese unit. He showed he could work with men from other nations, and the unit's performance and preparation improved while he was adviser.

## Back Home

Back at home, the equally explosive civil rights movement was in full swing. Martin Luther King Jr. and other civil rights activists organized campaigns demanding equality for black Americans. During one such campaign in Birmingham, Alabama—where Alma Powell lived with her parents—the demonstration turned violent. Local police forces used attack dogs, tear gas, and clubs to break up civil rights marches, and the bombing of a Birmingham church killed four little girls.

*Armed with attack dogs, policemen watch over a civil rights demonstration. One demonstration in the city where Alma Powell lived turned violent.*

Alma's father rarely let his shotgun out of his sight during these heated weeks.

As tumultuous as life in Birmingham was at the time, Alma never mentioned the civil rights turmoil in her letters to Colin. She did, however, write with other exciting news to share—the arrival of their first child. Michael Kevin Powell was born on March 23, 1963, and Alma immediately dispatched a letter to her husband notifying him of the baby's birth.

As the couple had agreed before Colin left for Vietnam, Alma wrote "Baby Letter" in bold letters across the envelope. When the letter arrived at headquarters in Vietnam, the clerk was to immediately radio Colin with the news. However, the clerk mistakenly shoved it underneath a huge pile of paperwork on his desk and forgot about it.

Almost two weeks after his son's birth, Powell received a letter from his mother that included the sentence, "Oh, by the way, we are absolutely delighted about the baby."[35] A frantic Powell, still unsure whether he was the father of a boy or a girl, contacted headquarters by radio and ordered them to search for the baby letter from his wife. A clerk finally located it and read Powell the happy news.

## Wounds and Untruths

The joy of being a new father was interrupted by the harsh reality of Vietnam. On July 23, 1963, Powell and a group of soldiers headed through the jungle to a nearby army camp for a brief rest period. During the trek there, the ground beneath Powell's right foot suddenly gave way and he stepped onto the sharp tip of a *punji* stick. *Punji* sticks were one of the Vietcong's methods of terrorizing the South Vietnamese and American troops. The guerrilla soldiers would dig small pits, wedge bamboo sticks in the bottom with the sharp ends pointing straight up, smother the tips with animal dung, then cover the pit with branches. When a soldier stepped onto one of the sticks, the point would penetrate the foot and the dung would spread poison through the wound.

No one else saw Powell step onto the stick, which had passed through the instep of his foot and emerged out the top. He wrenched his foot free, grabbed a branch as a makeshift cane, and hobbled on. Within twenty minutes Powell's swollen foot hurt so much that he could barely move, but he managed to make it to the army camp.

A medic took one look at the hugely swollen and purple foot and radioed for a helicopter to evacuate Powell. He was flown to a hospital in Hue, where a doctor forced a medicine-soaked cloth in one end of the wound, yanked it out through the top, then pulled it back and forth inside the wound as if he were shining shoes. Powell nearly fainted from the pain, but the treatment saved his foot. Within a few weeks he was able to resume duty.

Powell did not return to the A Shau Valley after his hospital stay. Instead, he was assigned to division headquarters in Hue and was given responsibility for instilling discipline and pride into a Vietnamese division. When he efficiently accomplished the task, Powell was honored by his superiors with a Bronze Star for outstanding achievement.

While stationed in Hue, Powell noticed a disturbing tendency among staff officers to misrepresent the truth in their reports. According to their records, the South Vietnamese were winning the war because, in official language, they had "secured" an increasing number of villages. Powell learned that a village was considered secure if the area was surrounded by protective fencing, had a handful of militia as guards, and if its local chief had not been killed in the last three weeks. The official reports described a far different war than what he experienced in the field. Powell later stated, "Nothing I had witnessed in the A Shau Valley indicated we were beating the Viet Cong. Beating them? Most of the time we could not even find them."[36]

## Reunited with Family

Powell returned to the United States at the end of 1963, eager to see his son for the first time. His joyous family reunion turned somber, however, when he realized what his family had endured while he was away. Powell knew little of the epoch civil rights events that had occurred in 1963, and he shuddered to think that his father-in-law had to guard the house that sheltered his wife and child with a shotgun. The sad irony of the situation—

that he placed his life on the line in Vietnam for rights which were simultaneously being denied to his wife and child—was not lost on the young officer:

> When I returned that Christmas, I was hit full force with what had happened in my absence. I was stunned, disheartened and angry. While I had been fighting in Vietnam alongside brave soldiers trying to preserve their freedom, in my own land a long-simmering conflict had turned into an open fight in our streets and cities—a fight that had yet to be won.[37]

Powell, however, had to put aside these feelings and focus on his new assignment. After spending time with Alma and Michael, he attended a one-month training course for the elite group of parachutists called Pathfinders. As the highest-ranking officer present, Powell was even in command during one training jump from a helicopter, although the other men present had much more experience in parachuting.

As they neared the jump area, Powell yelled to the men to make sure that their static lines, which automatically open the

## The Most Damaging Tragedy

Colin Powell had little sympathy for the draft system in place during the Vietnam War. Instead of fairly selecting those who would have to risk their lives in battle, the draft handed out numerous exemptions, normally to men whose families could afford to send them to college. Consequently, a higher proportion of poor youths, both black and white, served in the front ranks while wealthier males attended college. Powell claimed that this policy was a disgrace against democracy. In his autobiography, *My American Journey,* he explains his reasoning.

> I can never forgive a leadership that said, in effect: These young men—poorer, less educated, less privileged—are expendable, but the rest are too good to risk. I am angry that so many of the sons of the powerful and well placed and so many professional athletes (who were probably healthier than any of us) managed to wrangle slots in Reserve and National Guard units. Of the many tragedies of Vietnam, this raw class discrimination strikes me as the most damaging to the ideal that all Americans are created equal and owe allegiance to their country.

*During parachute training with the Pathfinders (pictured), Powell learned to never neglect details.*

chute, were hooked to the floor cable. A few moments later he shouted out the order a second time. He then stepped from man to man and checked each line. Surprisingly, one veteran sergeant had forgotten to hook his line. Had he jumped from the low-flying helicopter, he almost certainly would have plunged to his death.

That day Powell learned not to

> be afraid to challenge the pros, even in their own backyard. Just as important, never neglect details, even to the point of being a pest. Moments of stress, confusion, and fatigue are exactly when mistakes happen. And when everybody else's mind is dulled or distracted the leader must be doubly vigilant. "Always check small things" was becoming another of my rules.[38]

## Continuing Education

Powell's military education continued at a brisk pace. In August 1964 he entered a nine-month Infantry Officer Advanced Course at Fort Benning, which was a series of instructions to prepare captains for company command. Powell excelled in the classroom. One officer stated that Powell was "very impressive as a soldier. It was in his manner, his demeanor. There was no foolishness but he was very friendly. He was an intense, hard worker. People liked him." [39]

Yet some people still regarded Powell as inferior because of his race. While in Alabama with his wife, Powell was pulled over by a state police officer for speeding. Powell was driving a Volkswagen that sported a political sticker supporting Democratic president Lyndon Baines Johnson for reelection in 1964. The officer, who was handing out bumper stickers for Johnson's opponent, Senator Barry Goldwater, made no secret of his distaste for the driver. As Powell recalled, he "looked down at me, this young black soldier driving this foreign car with New York license plates and with the wrong bumper sticker. And he just looked down at me and said, 'Boy, you ain't smart enough to be around here. You need to leave.'" [40]

Again in 1964 Powell came face to face with bigotry when he stopped for a hamburger at Buck's Barbecue near Fort Benning. There, the waitress asked him if he were Puerto Rican or a visitor from Africa. When Powell replied that he was a Negro, the waitress said, "Well, I can't bring out a hamburger [to where white customers eat]. You'll have to go to the back door." [41] Rather than comply with the humiliating request, Powell drove away.

Other events in his personal and professional life continued apace. After daughter Linda was born on April 16, 1965, Powell, now a major, received orders to serve as an instructor at Fort Benning's infantry school. With the war in Vietnam dramatically escalating, the army needed more officers to supervise the half million men about to serve overseas. As one of the few officers with experience in Vietnamese warfare, Powell was asked to train others in the art of command during combat.

At each stage in his career, Powell compiled an enviable record and advanced faster than his classmates. As recognition, Powell was selected to attend the army's prestigious Command and General Staff College at Fort Leavenworth, Kansas, a nec-

*Soldiers train at Fort Benning, the infantry school in which Powell served as an instructor in 1965.*

essary step for those intent on rising through the ranks. The thirty-eight-week class taught men how to command a division of twelve thousand to fifteen thousand soldiers.

While at Leavenworth, Powell decided he wanted to attend graduate school to earn a master's degree. The army staff officer who inspected Powell's college grades, however, told him that he simply did not have an impressive enough academic record to enter graduate school. Instead of abandoning hope, Powell intended to prove his worth by doing the best he could at Fort Leavenworth. Out of a class of 1,244 officers, Powell finished second.

The hard work would reap dividends in 1968, when Vietnam again beckoned. Powell expected the call, though, since the army's expanded role in Southeast Asia required more officers. After a farewell dinner in July with Alma, Powell headed to the airport for a return to combat. He left his wife an envelope containing final instructions in case he were killed.

## A Second Tour

Powell returned to a different Vietnam than the one he had left in 1963. The nation's capital, Saigon, looked more American than Vietnamese. American soldiers, supplies, and vehicles jammed the city's streets. After a short time in Saigon, Powell traveled to his post in the countryside.

As executive officer of the Third Battalion, First Infantry of the Twenty-Third Infantry Division stationed near Chu Lai, Powell wielded enormous power in the battalion's day-to-day operations. While the overall commander supervised the soldiers in the field, Powell ensured that the paperwork was completed and the supplies were delivered. He performed so ably that his unit was chosen to represent the entire division in the annual inspection.

Powell remained in Chu Lai for only four months. The division commander, Major General Charles M. Gettys, had read an article in the *Army Times* about the recent graduating class from Fort Leavenworth and learned that he had the number-two graduate in his division. Gettys exploded: "I've got the number-two Leavenworth graduate in my division and he's stuck out in the boonies? I want him on my staff!"[42]

Powell later said that this move was one of the most important moves in his career. Instead of overseeing eight hundred men in the field, Powell would now help formulate the military plans for almost eighteen thousand soldiers and their support network of artillery, aircraft, and helicopters.

On November 16, 1968, Powell and Gettys boarded a helicopter to visit troops in the jungle. As the helicopter descended into the landing zone, a tiny circle hacked out of the trees, Powell noticed that the blades were shearing some branches. He worried that the zone, which allowed merely two feet of clearance at each side, was too tight for the chopper to land. A backdraft created by the trees rattled the craft, causing its blades to smack a thick tree trunk. In seconds the helicopter plunged thirty feet, crashing to the ground. As Powell recalls,

> One minute we were flying and the next we were dead weight, as the main rotor blades went instantly from 324

rpm (revolutions per minute) to zero. The helo dropped like an elevator with a snapped cable. I reflexively assumed the crash posture, head down, arms locked around my knees. I listened to the engine's futile whine for what seemed an eternity before we smashed into the ground.[43]

Powell shouted for everyone to get out of the craft before it exploded. He stumbled onto the ground but realized that others were not moving. He rushed back to the burning vehicle and found the barely conscious Gettys with a broken shoulder. He released the general's seat belt and dragged him to the nearby woods. Powell returned for Colonel Jack Treadwell, Gettys's chief of staff, and Ron Tumelson, Gettys's badly injured aide. Finally, Powell helped the pilot, who suffered from a fractured back, escape the damaged craft. He made these rescues despite the fact that he had a broken ankle, an action that earned him the Soldier's Medal for bravery in a noncombat situation.

## Honor Was Never the Issue

Colin Powell has never hidden from the fact that he is proud of his service in Vietnam and even prouder of those who fought with him. Some segments of society may have disdained Vietnam veterans, but he has made a point of bringing honor to their names. In his biography of Colin Powell, *Sacred Honor*, author David Roth quotes Powell's words delivered to Vietnam veterans in a Memorial Day speech at the Vietnam Wall following the Gulf War.

> You need no redemption. You redeemed yourself in the A Shau Valley. You redeemed yourself at Hue. You redeemed yourself at Dau Tieng, at Khe Sanh, in the South China Sea, in the air over Hanoi, or launching off Yankee Station, and in a thousand other places.

> The parades and celebrations are not needed to restore our honor as Vietnam veterans, because we never lost our honor. They're not to clear up the matter of our valor, because our valor was never in question. Fifty-eight thousand, one hundred and seventy-five names on this wall say that our valor and the value of our service were never in question.

## Bitter Lessons

When he was not serving in the field, Powell was often disturbed by much of what he saw. The United States wanted good press, so the military high command issued combat reports that inflated the number of Vietcong killed to make the American forces look good. Likewise, no clear sense of purpose had been spelled out by the generals conducting the war. The United States had sent its youth to fight in a land that did not seem to want them there, and the American public wanted a reason for this sacrifice. In the absence of that reason, antiwar sentiment dominated the headlines at home.

Powell's tour in Vietnam ended in 1969. Along with the Soldier's Medal, he received the Legion of Merit for his work with the division. When he returned to the United States, however, he experienced a different reception than in 1963. The military, which was revered during World War II, was now reviled. Some people spat at men in uniform and called Vietnam veterans baby killers. Powell's beloved army entered a period of disfavor among many in the nation.

Powell learned from the failure of Vietnam:

Many of my generation, the career captains, majors, and lieutenant colonels seasoned in that war, vowed that when our turn came to call the shots, we would not quietly acquiesce in half-hearted warfare for half-baked reasons that the American people could not understand or support. If we could make good on that promise to ourselves, to the civilian leadership, and to the country, then the sacrifices of Vietnam would not have been in vain.[44]

Years later, when Powell stood at the highest rank and ordered soldiers into a different war, he remembered these bitter lessons.

# Chapter 4

# "Excellence Is . . . a Prevailing Attitude"

FOLLOWING POWELL'S SECOND tour in Vietnam, he embarked on a new phase of his career that introduced him to the world of Washington, D.C., politics. In the 1970s he worked as an assistant and adviser for a series of political professionals who taught him how to maneuver in the often tricky political arena. In between these posts, Powell continued his rise to the top of the military's chain of command by successfully supervising men in the field. The recognition earned by his excellence in command, added to his hands-on political education, prepared Powell for what lay ahead.

## Graduate School

The initial step in this new phase of Powell's career occurred in the fall of 1969 when he attended graduate school at George Washington University in Washington, D.C. While most military officers chose to enter the international relations program, Powell opted for the school of business. He believed that in the future the army would require business management practices and computer proficiency. He also figured that a master's degree in business would be more attractive to companies after he retired from the army.

During the course of his graduate studies, Powell was promoted to lieutenant colonel, and he and Alma welcomed their third child, daughter Annemarie, on May 20, 1970. The family

## Three Keys to Powell's Effectiveness

Charles Duncan, Colin Powell's superior at the Department of Energy, appreciated the work Powell did for him. According to Duncan, his assistant's efficiency was no accident. Duncan explains his ideas in Howard Means's biography *Colin Powell*.

> He's a person who has extremely good skills at working with other people, and he's a very fast learner on things. He is totally committed to what he's doing. There's no limitation to hours or energy. He was there by six-thirty [in the morning] certainly, and by five-thirty if he needed to be. When he was my military assistant at the Pentagon, I'd be there by seven, and he would always be there before me and leave after me, and they were at least twelve-hour days.

also purchased a five-bedroom home in Dale City, a suburb of Washington, where Powell became active as a Sunday-school teacher and community leader in St. Margaret's Episcopal Church.

After earning his master's degree in business administration in July 1971, Powell reported to the Pentagon—the vast Washington, D.C., office building that houses the diverse military departments—where he worked for the army's assistant vice chief of staff, Lieutenant General William E. DuPuy. He loved this brief stint with DuPuy, who had a reputation as a brilliant, difficult taskmaster. Powell believed he could learn much from him.

With the war in Vietnam approaching its end, DuPuy foresaw that the army of the future would eventually need to cut back. The lieutenant general challenged his assistant: "Powell, I want you to take a couple of bright guys, go off into a corner, and start thinking the unthinkable. I want you to figure out how we would structure a five-hundred-thousand-man army."[45]

As the current army numbered more than one and a half million, Powell wondered how that could be accomplished. However, he and the other men batted around ideas and formulated a blueprint. From DuPuy, Powell learned to think the unthinkable and to plan ahead.

# White House Fellow

In November 1971, while still working for DuPuy, Powell was ordered by then Secretary of Defense Melvin Laird, to apply for a White House fellowship, a program designed for only the most able of military and political newcomers. It was an honor to be selected because the candidates would work at the top levels of government and learn from the most powerful politicians. Presidents, senators, and highly regarded journalists conducted seminars for the White House fellows, who gained a privileged glimpse of Washington politics.

When Powell learned that over one thousand applicants were vying for seventeen openings, he figured his chances of winning a fellowship were minimal. He was wrong, however. He won one of the coveted slots and was assigned to the Office of Management and Budget (OMB), the government agency that creates and supervises the federal budget. In this post, Powell worked with two men who would later influence his career: Caspar Weinberger, the head of the OMB, and Weinberger's deputy, Frank Carlucci.

*While working at the Office of Management and Budget, Powell was greatly influenced by Caspar Weinberger (back to camera) and Frank Carlucci (center).*

Powell earned the respect of the men he worked with as well as the respect of the other White House fellows. One fellow, James Bostic, said that Powell "had more experience than most of us. He helped people with the perspective of what was important and what was not. He was a nice guy. A consensus builder." [46]

Powell enjoyed the opportunity to observe government at its highest levels. At the OMB, he helped put together the federal budget and gained valuable experience resolving clashes between different offices. Still, he preferred to be in command of troops in the field, where he felt an officer belonged.

## Korea

Powell received his chance to return to the field in September 1973, when he was given command of the First Battalion, Thirty-Second Infantry stationed along the border between North and South Korea. Drug abuse, racial strife, and poor morale infected the battalion. In hopes of cleaning house, the division commander, Major General Hank Emerson, brought in Powell.

The new officer wasted little time implementing changes. Powell brought charges against the leaders of gang-like groups within the battalion, had others court-martialed, and gave increased responsibility to younger officers he felt he could trust. Powell kept the rest of the troops so busy that they had no time to think about problems. "We started running them every morning for four miles and working their butts off, and they were too tired to get in trouble, too exhausted to think about drugs. When nightfall came, they collapsed." [47]

There was one man whom Powell made a point of dealing with to serve as an example to the rest of the battalion. Corporal Biggs, a black soldier, had been telling his black comrades that white officers were out to get them. In addition, Biggs was involved in selling drugs. Powell called the corporal into his office. The soldier told Powell that the two should meet every day to discuss the serious morale problem, but Powell remarked that that would not be possible: "You see, Corporal, there's a plane at Osan and you are going to be on it today. That plane is going to Travis Air Force Base in California, and when you get off, some people will be waiting with your discharge papers. And they're going to put you out the gate." Biggs countered that Powell could not do that to him, to which Powell replied, "I've already done it. You're out of my battalion. Out of this brigade. Out of this division. Out of this man's Army. And you are unemployed."[48]

The other soldiers, especially the African American servicemen, were astonished that the new officer had so quickly and firmly removed a serious problem. From then on, every member knew not to mess with Powell, whom they started calling "Bro P."

To improve morale, Powell made certain that each month an outstanding soldier was nominated for the division's Soldier of the Month Award. This award was given to the soldier who best exemplified in his daily actions what the army hoped to instill in every individual—discipline, obedience, effort, and initiative. The selectees from each battalion then had to answer a series of challenging oral and written questions. Prior to Powell's arrival, a soldier was simply selected and then entered the competition with no preparation. Thus, no one from the battalion had ever won the award. Powell remedied that. The soldier would be chosen and then given assistance in preparing for the questions and other competitive portions of the contest. Though not a major part of the battalion's activity, Powell considered it essential. "If you are going to achieve excellence in big things, you develop the habit in little matters. Excellence is not an exception, it is a prevailing attitude."[49]

Powell enjoyed working for Major General Emerson, whom everyone called "Gunfighter" because of the six-shooter he wore at his belt during the Vietnam War. Emerson thought that every soldier was important, and to instill self-confidence, he organized a series of unusual athletic endeavors. Instead of regulation football or basketball, he instituted what he called combat football and combat basketball involving entire platoons. Eighty men might be on the field at any one time in Emerson's free-for-all versions. The major general proclaimed that if everyone played, everyone felt they contributed. "We want all of them to feel like winners,"[50] he told Powell and the other commanders. He felt so strongly that the men were more important than officers that when he handed over command of his division, he ordered his officers to face their men and salute them.

## A Friendly Sort

Though he rose to the highest levels of the military, Colin Powell could chat as easily with a local auto mechanic as he could with a president. In his biography of Powell, *Sacred Honor*, David Roth quotes Michael Powell's recollection of an incident while Powell commanded at Fort Leavenworth.

"We had this old house, built in the 1800s. It was a beautiful wood house. On Saturday morning everybody would be asleep, and Dad would come through with these people, giving a tour. He had just met them on the street. He'd seen them looking at the house and went out to explain things to them. Next thing, there would be these people walking by your room with strollers.

Not only did Powell learn from Emerson, but he also received the highest recommendation from the old general. In Powell, Emerson recognized talent in abundance and told his superiors that they had better promote him "as quick as the law allows." [51]

## Back in Washington

Others apparently agreed with Emerson's assessment, and after a nine-month stint analyzing weapons systems for the Defense Department in Washington, D.C., Powell was chosen to attend the nation's premier military educational institution, the National War College. Only those marked for higher command received invitations, and Powell excelled in a class filled with bright stars. One classmate, Harlan Ullman, said Powell was a "marked man. Everyone at the War College knew he was going to be chairman or whatever. He had that reputation, that aura, whatever, among his colleagues." [52]

Before graduating in 1976, Powell was promoted to colonel and was given command of the Second Brigade, 101st Airborne Division out of Fort Campbell, Kentucky. The famous "Screaming Eagles" of the 101st gained fame with their heroics at D day and the Battle of the Bulge in World War II, and to receive command of such an esteemed unit marked a man as one to watch.

Powell brought the same efficiency and organization to this job as he had to all of the others. He constantly drilled the twenty-five hundred men to whip them into fighting trim, and he made a point each afternoon to walk through the camp so that his troops could emerge from their quarters with any complaints.

According to Powell's division commander, Major General Jack Wickham, "Colin was the best brigade commander we had. He was best in his tactical knowledge, in his feel for soldiers, and his ability to communicate. He had a natural leadership style about him."[53]

Following his post in Kentucky, Powell returned to Washington to spend the next two and a half years as chief of staff to John Kester, the special assistant to Secretary of Defense Harold Brown. In his initial job interview with Powell, Kester informed Powell that he had done a background check on the officer "and I heard a lot of good things about you." Powell smiled, then replied, "Well, as a matter of fact, I checked you out, too, and it wasn't all good."[54] Kester figured that anyone willing to be as blunt as Powell deserved to be hired.

*Troops of the 101st Airborne Division take position after jumping off a helicopter during training. In 1976, Powell was given command of the Second Brigade of the 101st.*

Powell served as Kester's right-hand man. He decided who got in to see Kester and which phone calls were put through. Powell watched Kester outmaneuver some politicians and compromise with others, thus learning how the Washington political game worked. For instance, Kester rarely acted on a proposal put forward by someone else until that person had agreed to act favorably toward one of Kester's proposals. Powell was both fascinated and repulsed by the wheeling and dealing that occurred in the nation's capital.

In December 1978 Powell was promoted to brigadier general. At age forty-two Powell was the youngest general in the army. Though he wished to escape Washington and assume command of a division, Powell worked until 1981, when he was offered the assistant division command of the Fourth Mechanized Infantry Division at Fort Carson, Colorado, as the chief assistant to Secretary of Energy Charles Duncan.

## A Difficult Assignment

Some of Powell's friends warned him that the commanding officer at Fort Carson, Major General John Hudachek, was a difficult man who should never have been given command of a division. They urged Powell to decline the offer but, believing that he could endure whatever came along, Powell accepted.

Since a mechanized unit fought with tanks, Powell took a course to qualify as an expert tank gunner. Although Powell was not required to undertake the training, he thought it would make him better able to give orders to his soldiers if he understood what their jobs entailed.

While he experienced few difficulties with his subordinates, Powell's quiet demeanor did not fit well with Hudachek's confrontational manner. Powell later wrote,

> General Hudachek's leadership style was that of a tough overseer. The job got done, but by coercion, not motivation. Staff conferences turned into harangues. Inspections became inquisitions. The endless negative pressure exhausted the unit commanders and staff. The 4th Mech was a capable ship, but not a happy ship.[55]

When his term with Hudachek ended, Powell was disappointed in the efficiency report filed by the general. Instead of a flattering summary, to which Powell was accustomed, Hudachek reported glaring deficiencies in Powell's management. Powell feared that the report would end his upward path, but he felt that he had performed very well, and if Hudachek thought differently, there was little he could do about it.

Though Powell did not realize it at the time, other generals ignored the negative efficiency report because they had been impressed with what they had observed of Powell when visiting Hudachek's post. For instance, General Richard G. Cavasos remarked to a companion following a meeting with Hudachek and his commanders, "Did you notice anything in that conference room today? The only one who dared say anything in Hudachek's presence was Powell. The rest of them were terrified."[56]

Powell's fears over the poor efficiency report completely evaporated in August 1982, when he was named the deputy commanding general of Combined Arms Combat Development at Fort Leavenworth, Kansas. The post developed blueprints for the weapons of the future.

## Family

Whether immersed in his military or political work, Powell always made time for Alma and their three children. Colin and Alma raised their son and two daughters according to certain principles. "We're going to teach you right, we're going to teach you wrong, and we're going to teach you responsibility. If you have a problem and you mess up, you can always come and see us. But when you come and see us, you better tell us what you did about it."[57] In other words, making a mistake was not the worse error—failing to take responsibility and correct it was.

The couple never used corporal punishment, but they relied instead on letting the children know of their joy or displeasure over a certain action or inaction. Powell's look and his voice alone could be intimidating. As his daughter Linda recalls, "My father is a gentle man, but, as a child, I remember being a little afraid of him—he was so big. He rarely raised his voice, but when he did, my heart would drop through my stomach."[58]

*Powell and his wife, Alma, taught their children the difference between right and wrong and to be responsible for their mistakes.*

Powell, who always had trouble sharing feelings with others, had few face-to-face discussions with his children. When his son, Michael, turned sixteen, for example, Powell wrote a long letter expressing his hopes for his son. He told Michael that the next four years would toss severe challenges his way, such as sex or drugs, and that he had to be ready. "Just remember that our philosophy is that we show you right from wrong, and the rest is up to you. You don't do things according to our wishes. *You* make the decision of whether it's right or wrong in accord with the ways that we taught you."[59] In his letter, he added that Michael should never

> be afraid of failure. Be more afraid of not trying. . . . Take chances and risks—not foolhardy actions but actions which could result in failure, yet promise success and great reward. And always remember that no matter how bad something may seem, it will not be that bad tomorrow.[60]

It was advice Powell would soon use, for he was about to face a series of political and military crises.

---

# Chapter 5

# "A Rare and Valuable Asset"

IN 1974 ALMA POWELL had written a note to her husband predicting that he would command large numbers of men in an important post. In the 1980s, her prediction came true.

## Senior Military Assistant

After being promoted to major general in June 1983, Powell reported to the Pentagon to serve as senior military assistant to Secretary of Defense Caspar Weinberger. Weinberger had remembered the bright young officer who had served as a White House fellow and now brought him into his office to coordinate daily meetings and conferences.

Weinberger and Powell established a close relationship. They so perfectly complemented each other that Pentagon workers talked of them almost as one person. When Weinberger left the country on one of his frequent overseas trips, Powell seemed to always be at his side. Weinberger placed enormous responsibility on Powell's shoulders, and his military assistant never failed to respond. "He has my admiration," said Weinberger of Powell. "He knows what he's talking about and he always knows all of the buttons to push."[61]

Though he juggled countless daily requests to see the secretary, Powell managed to keep most politicians happy. Those who attended Powell's meetings appreciated how the officer stated the meeting's purpose, kept participants to the point, and brought the conference to a speedy conclusion. From his confident manner and crisp recital of detail, Powell was usually the best prepared individual at any meeting.

Powell showed this during the first major crisis he coordinated for Weinberger: the October 1983 invasion of the Caribbean island of Grenada. The United States feared that Cuba was trying to spread its Communist influence in the tiny nation. When Grenada's ruler, Maurice Bishop, was killed by Communist insurgents, the U.S. government sent in a combined force of army paratroopers, marines, and navy SEALs to protect one thousand American medical students on the island.

Powell also helped plan the 1986 American air attack on Libya. Libya's ruler, Mu'ammar Gadhafi, had been supporting acts of terrorism around the world. In hopes of deterring him from future violent actions, American aircraft demolished numerous targets in Libya during a swift bombing raid. Though Gadhafi survived the incident, he ceased being a problem for the United States.

While Powell continued to prosper on the professional level, his personal life suffered a setback when his mother died of can-

*U.S. Marines advance into Grenada during the October 1983 invasion. Powell's coordination of the operation demonstrated his efficiency and attention to detail.*

cer in June 1984, six years after his father had passed away from the same disease. Powell, who learned the value of hard work and self-discipline from his parents, claimed, "Parents are the luck of the draw. With my mother and father, I could not have been luckier."[62]

## The Iran Contra Controversy

The most controversial episode of Powell's career occurred in 1985 with what became known as the Iran Contra Affair. At that time, the country of Iran needed weapons for its war with neighboring Iraq, and U.S. national security adviser John Poindexter recommended that the United States ship missiles to Iran in exchange for both money and the release of American hostages being held in the Mideast. The profit from the weapons sale would then be placed in a secret fund that had been established to aid the Contras, a group of rebels that was fighting against the pro-Communist government of Nicaragua. Though the U. S. Congress had forbidden assistance to the Contras, Poindexter and other officials in President Ronald Reagan's administration intended to quietly ignore its wishes.

When Powell read a memo about the illegal operation, he notified Weinberger. Both men believed that Poindexter's moves violated the Arms Export Control Act, concluded that it went against the wishes of Congress, and opposed further contacts with Iran.

President Reagan, however, favored the deal. When Powell received orders from the Central Intelligence Agency (CIA) to arrange the transfer of more than forty-five hundred missiles, he obeyed. Once the missiles were out of his jurisdiction, though, Powell felt obliged to express his views of the incident. In a memo to Poindexter, he argued that Congress should be notified of the deal.

A subsequent investigation following the operation's exposure in 1987 implicated a number of officials and led to the removal of Poindexter from his position. Though Powell was questioned about the deal, he was cleared of any wrongdoing and was praised for writing the memo to Poindexter. "He was

*Both Powell and Caspar Weinberger (top) believed that John Poindexter (bottom) violated the Arms Export Control Act when he traded missiles to Iran for money and hostages.*

the only White House official to tape our sessions," said the investigator. "I figured he knew Washington and wanted to get his full reply on the record."[63]

## Duty in Germany

In June 1986 Powell returned to field command, his first love. Though he excelled in Washington's complex political world, he preferred managing soldiers to politicians. With his appointment to command the V Corps in Frankfurt, Germany, Powell would supervise seventy-five thousand troops.

Before the move overseas, he and Alma studied the German language eight hours a day for three weeks. Since terrorist acts against American military installations in Germany were occurring with alarming frequency, Colin and Alma also completed a course in defensive driving. The couple learned how to safely speed around curves, quickly turn a car to go in the opposite direction, and how to slam into a car blocking the road.

With terrorism to consider, their home in Germany was also heavily fortified, including barbed wire around the entire complex and a guardhouse. One of the home's bathrooms had been converted into an armor-covered retreat where Powell and his family were to flee in case terrorists penetrated the building. Ultimately, terrorists did not prove to be a problem during Powell's stay, but he did face an awkward situation with German environmentalists.

In an effort to prevent the U.S. military from destroying German landscape, environmentalists planted one hundred trees in the middle of the American tank driving range. One of Powell's commanders wanted to respond by crushing the trees in the treads of his tanks, but Powell had them dug up and replanted in the post's housing area. He then arranged an Earth Day celebration, to which he invited the environmentalists, the local German press, and politicians. While the environmentalists chose not to attend, Powell scored a hit with the German press. He explained that "with a little imagination you can turn a knock into a boost."[64]

## Powell Behind the Scenes

It did not take Colin Powell long to make a favorable impression after being named the national security adviser. He quickly had to arrange a summit between Mikhail Gorbachev and President Ronald Reagan, and as Simeon Booker explains in his profile of Powell, "Black General at the Summit of U.S. Power," which appeared in the July 1998 issue of *Ebony* magazine, he performed with distinction.

> Described as virtually unknown outside the nation's capital and military circles, Powell nevertheless has been a key architect in planning the series of superpower summit meetings between President Reagan and the Soviet Union's Mikhail Gorbachev. He has regularly taken his place on the American side of the conference table along with the President and Cabinet members, and he and his wife, Alma, have been standouts at the social functions that followed the long hours of negotiations.

Powell had been in Germany barely six months when Washington again beckoned. Following the Iran weapons deal, President Reagan named Frank Carlucci to succeed Poindexter as national security adviser. Carlucci immediately asked that Powell be reassigned as his top assistant. When he called to offer Powell the position, though, Carlucci received a lukewarm response.

"Frank, you're going to ruin my career,"[65] stated Powell, who thought that the move would label him as a general who worked well in Washington but could not command in the field. Powell told Carlucci that only a direct order from his commander in chief, the president, would pry him out of Germany. When President Reagan called on December 12, 1986, and asked Powell to accept Carlucci's offer, Powell instantly obeyed.

## Deputy National Security Adviser

The role of the National Security Council is to gather all points of view on a particular issue, debate the matter until a consensus is reached, and then present that solution to the president. The president then accepts or rejects the idea.

*Although reluctant to serve as national security adviser, Powell complied when President Reagan (right) called and asked him to take the position.*

At his new post, Powell enacted wholesale changes in the way things had been run by his predecessors. He reorganized the staff so that each person clearly understood his or her responsibility. He emphasized that no secrets would be kept from anyone, and he stated that each would have a chance to speak out on issues:

> I am a great believer that the interagency works best when everybody has a chance to say his piece and get his positions out on the table [so] that when we forward the final decision package to the president or present it to him orally, everybody who played knows he has been properly represented and had his day in court.[66]

Powell provided exactly one hour for open discussion of an issue, at the end of which he declared what decision he would recommend to Carlucci. Vice President George Bush, who sat through a seemingly endless succession of unorganized meetings, loved Powell's method. "He'd run them and get them over with in a hurry. He was thorough, and he presented people's positions very, very fairly and objectively as national security types have to do. He was crisp and strong in the way he put on the meetings, even with the President."[67]

Powell's changes helped restore flagging morale on the security council staff. As one aide stated, "The bickering and immobility that characterized the early years have disappeared. Colin's thoroughly professional and seems able not only to grasp the major policy issues but to detect dissonance [disagreement]. He operates in a low-key, unobtrusive manner."[68]

## A Family Crisis

Powell's Washington moves were interrupted on June 27, 1987, by a call from Germany informing him that his son, who had entered the army, had been injured in a jeep accident. The jeep in which he was riding had swerved to avoid an oncoming truck, flipped over and tossed Michael to the road, then crashed onto him as it bounded away. Michael, who suffered a crushed pelvis, broken back, and massive internal injuries, was rushed to a hospital, where doctors initially gave him little chance for survival.

The Powells flew to Germany to be with their son. Stunned at their first sight of Michael—swollen almost beyond recognition and hooked up to life support systems—they arranged for him to be flown to Walter Reed Army Medical Center in Washington, D.C., where they knew he would receive the best treatment available. Powell remained by his son's bedside for hours, whispering in Michael's ear over and over that he would make it. Unfortunately, Michael had to endure tremendous pain, because the amount of morphine needed to reduce the pain would have killed him.

Michael faced a series of operations and underwent rehabilitation from June 1987 until the following March, when he was finally released. Although he had to retire from the army with a 100 percent disability, he had defeated the odds by surviving.

## National Security Adviser

In November 1987 Frank Carlucci was promoted to secretary of defense, and President Reagan appointed Powell to replace him as national security adviser. For the first time in his Washington career, Powell occupied a top position.

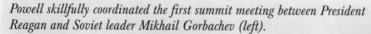

*Powell skillfully coordinated the first summit meeting between President Reagan and Soviet leader Mikhail Gorbachev (left).*

During his first month on the job, Powell successfully coordinated the first of three summit meetings between Reagan and Soviet leader Mikhail Gorbachev, who hoped to sign agreements reducing the number of nuclear weapons in both countries. In the initial summit meeting, Gorbachev agreed to on-site inspections that would ensure that both the United States and the Soviet Union were dismantling nuclear sites. Powell's skillful organization produced a smoothly run affair and impressed diplomats from both sides.

As the national security adviser, Powell recommended policies to the president. He never shied from presenting unpopular views if he thought they were correct, and the president knew that he could always count on Powell for the truth. President Reagan stated, "I have always been appreciative of Colin's candid assessment of situations. Finding someone who will talk straight to you in Washington is a rare and valuable asset. But to find someone who is straightforward and loyal is invaluable."[69]

## A Commitment to Equality

As the first African American to hold such a lofty governmental post, Powell felt a responsibility to do well. He also felt a responsibility to publicize the contributions made to the military by fellow African Americans. In speeches, Powell pointed out that George Washington commanded five thousand black soldiers in the American Revolution, that six hundred served with Andrew Jackson in the War of 1812, and that almost two hundred thousand joined the military in the Civil War. On his office wall he hung pictures of Henry Flipper, the first black cadet to graduate from West Point, and Brigadier General Benjamin O. Davis, the country's first black general.

At one White House dinner a black waiter walked near Powell and said, "I just want to thank you and say it's been good to see you here. I was in World War II, and I fought all the way from North Africa to Italy." Powell instantly grabbed the waiter's hand and said, "Brother, I ought to be thanking you!"[70]

Powell asserted that of all of the institutions in the United States, the military was the most democratic. Black and white advanced because of talent, not color, and he believed that the army offered a superb life. He claimed that he was never looked down on by anyone in the military because of his color. "What my color is is somebody else's problem, not mine. People will say, 'You're a terrific black general.' I'm trying to be the best *general* I can be."[71]

He succeeded. As White House colleague Tom Griscom mentioned, "No one ever thinks of Colin as being black; they think of him as being good."[72]

Powell's belief that each man is another's equal was tested in 1988 when his son, Michael, announced his intention to marry a white woman. At first the Powells worried about the problems their son would face with an interracial marriage, but the example of Colin's sister and her husband, Norm, eased their concern. Michael Powell and Jane Knott were married on October 1, 1988.

## Forces Command

During this time, Powell's professional life was experiencing dramatic changes. In November, when George Bush won the 1988 presidential election, he informed Powell that he preferred to have his own adviser heading the National Security Council. As reward for his loyalty, Powell received a promotion to four-star general and was placed in charge of Forces Command near Atlanta, Georgia.

### How to Make a Decision

Those who occupy a position of command must know how to make decisions. Colin Powell combines intelligence and instinct when making a decision, as he explains in a May 23, 1998, interview for the Academy of Achievement website.

One of my little rules is, you get all the facts you can. You get all of the analysis you can. You grind it up in your mental computer and then, when you have all the facts available to you, go with your instinct. . . . Built into each of us is a little calculator that can make judgments that will never appear on a piece of paper. And sometimes you just know something's right—you can't prove it to anybody—or you know something's wrong. Little ethical circuit breakers you carry around inside of you, or little right and wrong circuit breakers you carry around inside of you. So, I go with my instinct a great deal.

*After George Bush (right) was elected president in 1988, Powell was promoted to four-star general and given charge of Forces Command.*

Given responsibility for the defense of the continental United States, this is the largest command an army general can receive.

For a brief time before accepting the Atlanta posting, Powell considered retiring. A literary agent explained that he could easily earn $1 million on the lecture tour and through writing, and the commercial market eagerly sought someone with his credentials in politics and the military. Powell compiled a list of reasons why he should retire from the army and another listing reasons why he should remain. While his reasons for staying in the army filled the page, the sole argument supporting his retiring was money, so he remained.

During Powell's brief tenure with Forces Command, he predicted that much of Communist-controlled Eastern Europe would soon be free from Soviet control, and he believed the Middle East was a potential hot spot. He did not realize at the time how accurate he was, nor how active a role he would play in those places in the next few years. Once again, within months of taking his Atlanta post, Powell was on the move. In October 1989 he was named to the top military position in the nation—chairman of the Joint Chiefs of Staff.

# Chapter 6

# "Go in Big, and End It Quickly"

SINCE HIS FIRST assignment as a platoon leader in West Germany, Colin Powell had swiftly risen through the ranks of the military. At each step he carried out his responsibilities with confidence and gained the respect of his subordinates and fellow workers. His new post as chairman of the Joint Chiefs of Staff offered the biggest professional challenge of his career.

## Immediately into the Fray

The Joint Chiefs of Staff consists of the heads of the army, navy, marines, air force, and a chairman. The chairman serves a two-year term and conducts meetings with the joint chiefs to decide military policies and make recommendations to the president. The fifty-two-year-old Powell would not only be the youngest man to occupy the chairman's position, he would also be the first African American and the first soldier not to have graduated from one of the military academies such as West Point.

On Powell's first day he received an urgent phone call that Panamanian dictator Manuel Noriega might be overthrown in a revolution. President Bush wanted Noriega's government out of power because of Noriega's involvement in the drug trade and because the dictator ignored the Panamanian people's democratic rights. When Bush asked Powell if he should send in U.S. soldiers to help the rebel leaders overturn Noriega, however, Powell recommended that he wait. Powell feared that the rebel leaders did not have sufficient support from their fellow countrymen and had few intentions of implementing democratic

*Powell recommended a cautious approach when President Bush asked if U.S. troops should help overthrow Panamanian dictator Manuel Noriega (pictured).*

measures themselves. When the poorly executed revolution failed miserably, lasting only three hours, Powell's advice gained him credibility with his new boss.

A more serious Panamanian crisis erupted two months later. On December 16, 1989, a marine was killed in Panama and a navy officer and his wife were beaten. When Powell recommended military action to protect American citizens in Panama, Bush ordered him to draw up plans to send in a military force to remove Noriega. Powell assembled more than twenty thousand soldiers for Operation Just Cause, including U.S. Army Rangers, paratroopers, Special Forces, navy SEALs, and the elite Delta Force, a unit of highly trained men skilled in quick attacks.

The December 20 invasion of Panama was Powell's first experience in sending large numbers of troops into battle. As some would inevitably be killed, the burden of his decision wore on him in the hours immediately preceding the military action:

> I was going to be involved in conducting a war, one that I had urged, one that was sure to spill blood. Had I been right? Had my advice been sound? What if the icy weather in the States hampered the airlift? How would we then support the troops already in Panama? What would our casualties be? How many civilians might lose their lives in the fighting? Was it all worth it?[73]

## Long-Distance Connection

One of the amazing facets of modern warfare is the ability of a commander like Colin Powell to follow the progress of soldiers in the field.
During the American invasion of Panama, the super elite Delta Force
rescued an American citizen, Kurt Muse, from a prison before Manuel
Noriega could make good on his promise to execute the American in
the event of an invasion. In his autobiography, *My American Journey*,
Powell records the transmission he heard in Washington as a member
of Delta Force described the action. Powell stated that the action,
which lasted only six minutes, seemed an eternity to him. He could
do nothing but listen as the action unfolded before his ears.

> Delta Force landing on the roof of Modelo Prison. . . . Delta has
> killed the guards. . . . Delta Force in. . . . Kurt Muse out of his
> cell. . . . Delta Force leaving in helicopters from the roof. It's okay.
> No! The helo is taking fire. It's hit! It's coming down! No, it's going
> down in the street . . . it's hit . . . it's down . . . they're okay. . . .

Powell's role during the attack was to explain the action's
purpose to the American public. When he spoke on television,
Powell successfully conveyed a sense of calm efficiency, reas-
suring the American people that the military knew what it was
doing. By doing this, he hoped to restore the trust in the military
that had been eroded by the tumultuous Vietnam years.

In that first day, American troops easily overcame the opposition mounted by Panamanian soldiers and forced Noriega
into hiding. The smoothly run invasion, which was the first de-
cisive military victory for American troops since World War II,
lasted less than two weeks. Noriega finally surrendered to
American troops in January 1990, and a new leader was installed. Powell gained high marks for both the operation's efficiency and his ability to connect with the public on television.

## A New Military

In his initial days as chairman, Powell established guidelines
with his staff and set goals for the coming months. Due to diminished danger from the economically unstable Soviet Union
in Europe and North Korea in Asia, Powell felt that forces could
be decreased in both areas and ordered his staff to plan to reduce the military by as much as one-third. He predicted that the

American military would need to streamline its forces and focus on a number of specially trained regional units rather than one huge military. He intended that the American military would be smaller, more efficient, and able to counter a crisis wherever one flared. "The wake-up call can come at any moment, and we don't put our friends and interests on hold,"[74] he asserted.

To those who disagreed with America's involvement in other nations' affairs, Powell asserted that it was one of the responsibilities of being a superpower. "One of the fondest expressions around is that we can't be the world's policeman. I certainly agree that we should not go around saying we are the world's policeman. But guess who gets called when suddenly someone needs a cop?"[75]

Powell intended to create what he called Base Force, a reduced military that still retained the capability of responding to threats in two different sections of the globe. Knowing that he would receive severe opposition from the military chiefs, Powell

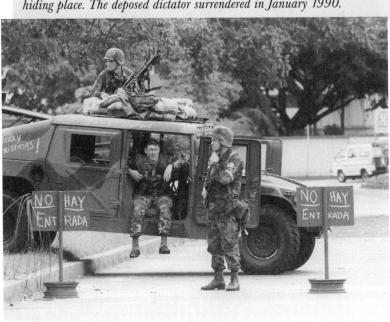

*During Operation Just Cause, American soldiers wait outside Noriega's hiding place. The deposed dictator surrendered in January 1990.*

## We Are the Best

Colin Powell contends that people can perform to the maximum of their abilities only by believing that they are the best. He exhibited that philosophy when he trained troops in different field commands, and he mentioned it in numerous speeches and meetings. In his biography *Sacred Honor,* author David Roth included the following quote from Powell.

> Every soldier must take the battlefield believing his or her unit is the best in the world. Every pilot must take off believing there is no one better in the sky. Every sailor standing watch must believe there is no better ship at sea. Every Marine must hit the beach believing that there are no better infantrymen in the world. But they must also believe that they are part of a team, a joint team, that fights together to win. This is our history, this is our tradition, this is our future.

waited for the right moment to announce his proposals. He seized his opportunity when the Berlin Wall, which had separated Communist East Berlin from the democratic West Berlin for more than forty years, was torn down on November 10, 1989. With the power of Soviet communism on the decline, Powell went public with his plans.

## Background to War

Powell's efforts were halted almost before he started. Before he could seriously commit to military reduction plans, Powell's attention switched to the Mideast, where Iraq had begun to build up its military forces along its border with the oil-rich nation of Kuwait. Iraq had long claimed Kuwait as part of its nation, and this aggressive move concerned the United States. Iraq's dictator, Saddam Hussein, commanded the world's fourth-largest military machine, and he had placed almost half a million men, supported by numerous tanks and artillery pieces, near the border. Should Hussein gain control of Kuwait, he would gain valuable oil for his military machine and place his forces closer to even more oil fields in Saudi Arabia. Should Hussein control Saudi Arabia, he would possess 40 percent of the world's oil reserves, becoming the major power in the Mideast.

In response to rumors that Hussein planned to invade Kuwait, Saudi Arabia asked President George Bush for American military and financial aid. Bush ordered Powell and General H. Norman Schwarzkopf, the commander of U.S. military forces in the Mideast, to formulate plans for a potential offensive.

On August 2, 1990, Hussein ordered eighty thousand Iraqi soldiers into Kuwait, overrunning the tiny nation in days. Most nations of the world condemned Iraq's actions, and the United Nations called for Iraq's withdrawal. The United States and other nations blockaded Iraqi ports, ceasing all trade with the country.

Bush met with his advisers about the possibility of war. Powell, who had seen the military crippled by indecision in the Vietnam War, was determined to formulate a clearly defined purpose before any American troops set foot in the Mideast and, once war had been decided, to ensure that the politicians would commit the most potent force possible. In deciding whether to take action, Powell recommended that they consider whether American troops

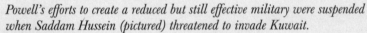

*Powell's efforts to create a reduced but still effective military were suspended when Saddam Hussein (pictured) threatened to invade Kuwait.*

were to push Iraq out of Kuwait, to destroy Hussein's war-making ability, or to invade Iraq and seize its capital, Baghdad. He explained that each step required a different level of troops and thus needed different amounts of time for preparation.

For his own part, Powell at first opposed military action in Kuwait. He feared the invasion would take so long that public support would dissipate. He also doubted that oil was worth the loss of lives, stating, "The American people do not want their young dying for $1.50 [for a gallon of] oil."[76]

Powell would later be criticized for his cautious stance. Some called him a reluctant warrior who wanted to avoid war, but he countered that he simply fulfilled his duty of presenting all possible courses to the president, who would then make the decision. Under no circumstance would he recommend going to war until he thought sufficient force had been committed to the endeavor.

A United Nations resolution outlining a course of military action freed Powell from any worry about the purpose of his mission. It stated that Allied forces were to free Kuwait from Iraqi control and made no mention of destroying Iraqi military capability or invading Iraq.

That feeling coincided with evolving American military objectives. As Powell wrote, "In none of the meetings I attended was dismembering Iraq, conquering Baghdad, or changing the Iraqi form of government ever seriously considered."[77] He added that while no one would have minded Saddam Hussein's death, that was never a priority.

Powell hoped that economic sanctions and the blockade of Iraqi ports would force Hussein out of Kuwait, but that hope quickly disappeared. It seemed more likely that Hussein would indefinitely remain in Kuwait, no matter what hardships his own people might suffer. During an October 30 White House meeting, Powell presented a plan to push Hussein out of Kuwait with an American contingent of army, navy, and marine units supported by a coalition of other nations. He proposed that a large-scale bombing offensive would start in the middle of January 1991, followed by a ground assault in February. President Bush agreed to issue an ultimatum to Hussein insisting that he must leave Kuwait by January 15, 1991, or expect severe repercussions.

## Preparations for War

U.S. soldiers, aircraft, ships, and material began pouring into Saudi Arabia only five days after Hussein's army crossed into Kuwait. From November 1990 through January 1991, hundreds of ships and transport planes moved thousands of aircraft and soldiers into Saudi Arabia and surrounding regions.

Powell understood the value of possessing overwhelming force. He wanted his men and women to go into Kuwait, remove the Iraqi forces, and be done as soon as possible before public support waned:

> The American people want their interests protected and they want their values protected and they are willing to help others who are in need and for whom we may have some responsibility. But at the same time, being very reasonable, practical people, they hope we will do it quickly, efficiently, and successfully. The quicker you can do it, the better off you are. That means making sure you have clear instructions for what you are being asked to do and then putting in the necessary force to do it.[78]

In preparing for war, Powell found himself in the middle between General Schwarzkopf, who wanted additional troops and time before starting ground operations, and President Bush, who

*U.S. troops arrive in Saudi Arabia in response to Iraq's invasion of Kuwait. Powell realized that overwhelming force would be needed to remove the Iraqis.*

wanted to kick off an offensive while public support remained strong. To guarantee that American troops outnumbered the Iraqis in both men and firepower, Powell dispatched even more troops than Schwarzkopf requested. "I beefed up his request for additional fighter squadrons. Aircraft carriers? Let's send six. We had paid for this stuff. Why not use it? What were we saving it for? We had learned a lesson in Panama. Go in big, and end it quickly. We could not put the United States through another Vietnam." [79]

## Instant Thunder

When the January deadline passed without Hussein pulling back, the United States implemented Instant Thunder, the first step in answering Hussein's bold advances. The one-month bombing campaign was designed to destroy Iraqi communications, bridges, tanks, troops, artillery, and its air force.

In the early morning hours of January 17 army helicopters bombed Iraqi radar sites, creating an electronic hole through

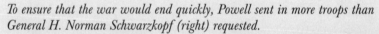

*To ensure that the war would end quickly, Powell sent in more troops than General H. Norman Schwarzkopf (right) requested.*

which successive waves of American planes flew. Repeated air attacks over the next month reduced Iraqi strength, but Hussein's troops remained in Kuwait. When the American public wondered why Hussein could not be eliminated, Powell asked them, on national television, to trust the American strategy. He received a favorable response in the press, but Powell knew that if the war in Kuwait lasted too long, he could quickly lose that support.

In the days before the ground offensive, Powell warned President Bush about the unpleasant aspect of warfare. The air war had been, in many ways, a video war. Pilots fired missiles at targets that showed up on radar screens, and cameras installed on the missiles plotted their course as they streaked toward their targets. Americans at home watched on television as missiles tore into Iraqi positions.

A ground war, however, pitted human against human. Powell said to Bush,

> When a battalion runs into a firefight, you don't lose a pilot or two, you can lose fifty to a hundred men in minutes. And a battlefield is not a pretty sight. You'll see a kid's scorched torso hanging out of a tank turret while ammo cooking off [firing] inside has torn the rest of the crew apart. We have to brace ourselves for some ugly images.[80]

Powell, who slept in his office every night of the operation, struggled with his thoughts in the early hours before the invasion launched. He knew he was sending some soldiers to their deaths, "both the young men and women you send in to do it, and the young men and women that they will kill on the other side."[81]

## The Hundred-Hour War

At 4:00 A.M. on February 24, U.S. forces crossed into Kuwait to commence Operation Desert Storm. While one thrust occupied Iraqi troops along the border, a second arm swung westward to cut off lines of support from Iraq and to slam shut any possibility of Hussein's troops retreating homeward. American units advanced sixty miles into Kuwait on the first day and captured ten thousand Iraqi soldiers. Some soldiers even broke through Iraqi lines and headed toward Kuwait City, which was not an early objective. Hussein was forced to pull back his troops to the line they had occupied before they invaded Kuwait.

While American marine and army units continued an aggressive advance on the second day, an Iraqi missile demolished an American barracks in Saudi Arabia, killing twenty-eight soldiers, including female troops. On the third day of Operation Desert Storm, ecstatic soldiers liberated Kuwait City while other contingents moved closer to Iraq. In the course of only three days, twenty-seven of forty-two Iraqi divisions had been either overrun or destroyed.

Throughout the short conflict, Powell excelled at getting his message across to the American public. He energized the nation with his blunt summation of American plans: "Our strategy to go after this army is very, very simple. First, we're going to cut it off, and then we're going to kill it."[82] One reporter compared Powell on television to a kindly professor who calmly explained intricate details in simple fashion. Powell recognized that when he spoke in front of the television cameras, he talked to four separate groups—the American people, foreign nations, his troops, and the enemy. He made sure to fashion his statements to achieve his desired effect.

By day four the war appeared to be winding down. Iraqi troops were fleeing in disarray along the last major escape route from Kuwait City to Iraq, a four-lane highway labeled "the Highway of Death." Burning Iraqi vehicles and dead soldiers littered the road for miles as American aircraft swooped down unopposed. Powell was concerned that televised images of the destruction would appear more a slaughter than warfare and consulted with Schwarzkopf about ending the offensive. With his field commander in agreement, Powell advised President Bush that the war could be ended. At midnight on the fourth day, hostilities ceased, and the Hundred-Hour War drew to a close.

## Controversy and Acclaim

At a cost of 147 Americans killed in combat and another 236 dead from accidents, U.S. forces halted Iraqi aggression and restored pride in the military. But whether the war with Iraq

*A helicopter herds a column of surrendering Iraqi soldiers. It was later estimated that one half of Iraq's army escaped destruction or avoided capture.*

should have ended remained a matter of both confusion and controversy in its immediate aftermath.

On March 1 the Central Intelligence Agency estimated that one half of the Iraqi army survived Operation Desert Storm, even though many fled directly in front of halted American units. Even President Bush seemed to doubt the conflict's conclusion. Only two days after the cease-fire, Bush mentioned to a reporter that in World War II "there was a definitive end to that conflict. And now we have Saddam Hussein still there—the man that wreaked this havoc upon his neighbors."[83]

In April political reporter Bob Woodward published his book on the Persian Gulf conflict, *The Commanders,* in which he asserted that Powell had opposed any military action against Iraq. General Schwarzkopf added fuel to the flames by stating in a television interview that he recommended that American forces continue their successful drive and head into Iraq instead of stopping in Kuwait.

Powell and his supporters refuted the arguments by repeating that the goal had never been to overthrow Hussein—it was to evict the Iraqi army from Kuwait. As Powell replied in an interview,

"When after forty-three days [of military operations], which included a four-day ground war we reached the point where those
objectives had been accomplished, the President ordered us to
stop offensive operations."[84]

Part of the responsibility for the initial controversy rested
with George Bush. During the war he had gone out of his way
to picture Hussein as America's archenemy. When the war
ended, the American people could not understand why Hussein
was still in power.

President Bush telephoned Powell about the criticism.
"Colin, pay no attention to that nonsense. Don't worry about it.
Don't let 'em get under your skin."[85] Bush backed his words in
early May by publicly praising Powell's performance in the Gulf
War. On May 23, 1991, Bush reappointed Powell to a second
two-year term as chairman.

In April the U.S. Congress authorized money for two special
gold medals to honor Powell and Schwarzkopf. The action was
the beginning of an outpouring of gratitude from the nation to
its returning soldiers. Parades wound through Washington, D.C.;
Chicago; and New York City, where thousands of people show-
ered Powell and others in ticker tape. Following the disaster in
Vietnam, where few parades welcomed home the soldiers, the
joyous celebrations encouraged old warriors like Colin Powell:

> We had given America a clear win at low casualties in a
> noble cause, and the American people fell in love again
> with their armed forces. The way I looked at it, if we got
> too much adulation for this one, it made up for the ne-
> glect the troops had experienced coming home from
> those other wars.[86]

---

# Chapter 7

# "You Did Well by America"

W ITH THE GULF WAR over, Powell turned to other important matters. During his second term as chairman of the Joint Chiefs of Staff, he implemented changes to adapt the military to a post-war world and used his position as a platform on which to speak out on different issues.

## Other Concerns

Powell recommended his Base Force notion to the president in February of 1992. In light of the diminished need for armed forces with the collapse of the Soviet Union, Powell proposed to reduce the total number of troops while maintaining enough military strength so that the armed forces could simultaneously fight two major regional conflicts. In this manner, should one conflict erupt, the United States would still retain enough power to halt aggression elsewhere, but the nation would be freed from the obligation to support the vast military machine that existed through the cold war years with the Soviet Union. President Bush went along with Powell's ideas and by early 1992 some military bases in Europe and the United States were closed, and the number of soldiers decreased.

But while some military bases were closing, the United States appeared to be drawing closer to intervening in two areas: the African nation of Somalia, where widespread hunger and fighting among rival tribal clans had dissolved any sense of order, and the European nation of Bosnia, where ancient hatreds were spawning ghastly killings and mass slaughter.

*Seeing no valid reason to intervene, Powell opposed sending American troops into Somalia and Bosnia. He believed that the problems in both countries needed to be solved by political means.*

Powell recommended against action in both cases. Though the United States did eventually commit troops to the two regions, he saw no clearly defined reason for intervention. He did not believe that an American military presence could install democracy in Somalia, where hundreds of years of tribal feuds dominated, and he argued that ethnic groups in Bosnia had clashed for thousands of years. He believed that instead of military action, which he thought would require a much larger commitment than the nation wanted, both issues needed a political settlement.

Another sensitive area for the military involved the issue of homosexuality. Like many of his fellow officers, Powell strongly argued against allowing gays in the military. He contended that the military required soldiers to live and sleep in the same barracks or same cramped quarters aboard ship, and placing gays in such a situation constituted a threat to the privacy rights of other soldiers.

Newspaper editorials criticized Powell's stand on the issue and wondered how an African American could support a policy that denied another group rights offered to the nation at large. Powell countered that the two issues were not similar. "Requiring people of different color to live together in intimate situations [sleeping in the same barracks] is far different from requiring people of different sexual orientation to do so."[87]

Powell proposed that when a person enlisted in the military, he or she simply not be asked about sexual preference. As long as the individual did not subsequently disclose that he or she was gay, there would be no problem. Congress eventually approved the policy, which became known as the "don't ask, don't tell" policy.

In another area, Powell attempted to use the military to bring hope to inner-city youth. He had benefited from the

*Despite Powell's recommendations, U.S. troops were sent into Bosnia. Here soldiers look over a mass grave containing hundreds of Bosnian corpses.*

## How About the Military?

Throughout his career Colin Powell has been one of the most avid spokesmen praising the benefits of the army. He believes that every young person can gain valuable experience by enlisting. What does he find so beneficial? He expressed his thoughts in "Colin Powell, Superstar: Will America's Top General Trade His Uniform for a Future in Politics?" an interview with *U.S. News & World Report.*

What is it that we give young men and women when they come in that might be lacking outside? It's some structure, expectations, caring, role modeling, recognition, reward, punishment—meaning there are consequences for poor behavior and not meeting standards. And then all the help in the world to meet those standards.

ROTC program and believed that thousands of high-school students might do the same. With pride in the military restored by the successful Desert Storm operations, Powell instituted a Junior ROTC program and offered it to high schools. Junior ROTC hired retired military officers to teach students citizenship, military history, map reading, and other subjects. While some educators decried the move as an attempt to lure students into the military, Powell emphasized the benefits of bringing discipline, hard work, and a sense of family to troubled kids.

## A Role Model

Though he works with adults day after day, Powell considers his labor on behalf of young people to be of the utmost importance. His status as a hero after Desert Storm gives him a credibility that he uses to convey different messages. Of the three hundred letters he receives each day, Powell answers each one that is written by a child. At the bottom of each response he always adds, "Stay in school."[88]

When students ask him how he succeeded, Powell has a quick reply: "Worked like a dog! That's how I did it. I work very, very hard. I always have." He adds, "Everywhere I have gone, I've tried to make that point. I don't know successful people who don't work hard. Success is hard work."[89]

He also tells young people to select something they enjoy and turn that into a career. One time his daughter Linda mentioned that she wanted to become an actress. Rather than discouraging her, Powell related that he had just seen a cousin of hers "who is an engineer. I asked her how she liked it. She didn't seem to be at all excited about being an engineer. I think you should do what's going to make you happy."[90]

Powell also delivers blunt advice to young African Americans: Do not make excuses or accept excuses. Regarding young blacks, he says,

> Even though they are trapped in some structural situations that are hard to break out of, they've got to try and break out of it. They have no choice. They can't just sit there and go down with it. And so the message I give young people as I talk in high schools essentially says, "Do not let the fact that you're a minority or that you came from a different background or that you are trapped structurally somewhere serve as an anchor to keep you down. You've got to swim against it, you've got to climb against it."[91]

## Retirement from the Military

In September 1993 Colin Powell donned his uniform as a military officer in the U.S. Army for the final time. After stopping by his office, Powell headed to the White House, where he and President Bill Clinton chatted for an hour. Powell told the president that he intended to take care of his family's financial security—a $6-million book contract for his memoirs guaranteed that—and then settle into some favorite hobbies. Powell then ate lunch with the military chiefs, who surprised the general by bringing in former president George Bush for the affair.

A formal retirement ceremony took place at Fort Myer outside of Washington, D.C., with an array of family, friends, fellow officers, and politicians in attendance, including Caspar Weinberger, George Bush, and President Clinton. The president told the audience that Powell "clearly has the warrior spirit and the judgment to know when it should be applied in the nation's

*President Clinton awards the Medal of Freedom to Powell during the general's retirement ceremony. Powell was also presented with an old Volvo automobile that his friends had purchased for him.*

behalf. . . . I speak for the families who entrusted you with their sons and daughters. . . . You did well by them, as you did well by America." [92]

Clinton then presented Powell with the retirement gift for which his friends had contributed: a rusted-out 1966 Volvo automobile. Knowing how much Powell loved to tinker with old Volvos, his friends had searched until they found the right vehicle.

A military career that began thirty-five years earlier came to an emotional end. Colin Powell, citizen, left the podium to embrace his wife.

## A Civilian at Last

Powell laughs that reality intruded the next morning when he walked downstairs for breakfast with Alma. She informed him that the sink had backed up and spilled water all over the floor, and his first thought was to call the military engineer to repair the sink before suddenly realizing that he could no longer do that. "I spent my first civilian morning crouched under a dripping sink."[93]

Besides writing his memoirs and delivering speeches on the lecture circuit, Powell turned to hobbies to occupy some of his spare time. He watched old movies and read histories and biographies, but mainly he stepped into his garage, turned on some music, and worked on the engine of his Volvo.

Official duties beckoned at times. In December 1993 Queen Elizabeth II of England knighted Powell, and the following September he was asked by former president Jimmy Carter to accompany him to Haiti on a peacekeeping mission. In December 1994 one of President Clinton's aides inquired whether Powell would like to be secretary of state, but he declined.

His major professional enjoyment since retirement has been the work he has done in conjunction with America's Promise. The organization unites the resources of business and government for the assistance of young people. Mentoring programs and proper health care are just a few of the items stressed by the group.

## Grease Up to His Arms

Colin Powell's favorite way to relax is to disappear into his garage to work on the latest in a string of worn out Volvos. For hours at a time he and his longtime military driver, Otis Pearson, can quietly figure out how to put a reluctant vehicle on the roads again. Local auto parts dealers are never surprised when Colin Powell, with grease covering his arms, walks in and asks for certain parts.

In his autobiography, *My American Journey*, Powell explains his love of auto repair.

> My idea of a good time is to disconnect every wire, tube, hose, cable, and bolt of an engine, unhook the driveshaft from the transmission, sling a chain around the engine, hook the chain to the rafters, and winch the engine out of the hood, as I stand there, grease-stained and triumphant.

America's Promise, along with Powell, chose a little red wagon as its symbol to emphasize the idea that every child needs to have a dream. He explains that the wagon is

> a perfect symbol of a nostalgic childhood. Every boy and girl ought to have a little red wagon that can pull along a kid brother, a kid sister, a heavy load, a dream. A little red wagon that one day could be a rocket ship, or another day it could be an ocean liner, but it's there to help you make your way through life. And it comes with a nice long black handle, so that an adult can reach down, grab it and help you. That's the symbol of America's Promise. I'm trying to make sure that every child in America has a little red wagon.[94]

Powell encourages parents and schools to combine efforts on behalf of their children. He contends that responsibility for the future rests on parents, schools, and students—parents must begin parenting, schools must begin teaching, and students must begin studying.

*During a fundraising event for America's Promise in New York, Powell stands with Mayor Rudolph Giuliani and singer Janet Jackson, who is holding the symbol of the organization.*

## Presidential Candidate?

One issue that has followed Powell into retirement is whether he will run for president. Many people stand ready to support him should he choose to run, but so far he has preferred to remain a private citizen.

The first rumblings started in 1987 when Frank Carlucci mentioned in *Time* magazine that Powell would make a perfect presidential candidate. The next year British prime minister Margaret Thatcher recommended to George Bush that he select Powell as his vice presidential running mate, but Bush turned to Dan Quayle instead.

The successful completion of Operation Desert Storm made Powell an even more attractive candidate. His cousin, federal judge James Watson, recalled attending a meeting of a Florida bar association shortly after Desert Storm. When the introductory speaker mentioned that Colin Powell was Watson's cousin, the entire audience rose and applauded.

Some Republican advisers urged Bush to replace Dan Quayle as his vice presidential candidate in 1992. The same year the other major political party, the Democrats, contacted Powell about the possibility of joining them. Powell replied, "I don't intend to step out of uniform one day and into partisan politics the next. Second, I don't even know what I am politically. And third, George Bush picked me up and stuck by me. I could never campaign against him." [95]

Political surveys at the time showed that Powell could make a strong run for president, even if he ran against the incumbent, Bill Clinton. Voters warmed to Powell's dignity, liked that he had restored faith and trust in the military, and valued that he seemed to rise above the dirty politics that many felt characterize politicians. They saw in him an example of the old-fashioned idea that, through hard work, anyone in America can succeed.

For all of his supporters, Powell had his critics. Some black militants claimed that he catered to the white establishment, and antiwar critics attacked him as being responsible for killing thousands of Iraqi civilians in the Gulf War. In addition, the specter of bigotry and prejudice lurked. People can state that they will vote for an African American candidate, but will they cast their ballot for that person in the secrecy of the voting booth?

Powell had not even indicated which political party he preferred. He agreed with the Republican stance on a strong military, order at home, and the importance of the family unit, but he felt uncomfortable with their lack of support for civil rights. On the other hand, the Democratic belief that government should develop costly assistance programs contradicted his experience that hard work reaps rewards.

Powell continues to believe that the nation needs to avoid dividing the population into ethnic groups, such as African Americans or Irish Americans, and instead place a renewed emphasis on the family. He reminds people of an interview during Desert Storm when a reporter asked an African American soldier if he would be frightened when the fighting began. With his fellow soldiers standing about, including whites, Hispanics, and other blacks, the soldier replied, "We'll do okay. We're well trained. And I'm not afraid. I'm not afraid because I'm with my family. This is my family and we'll take care of each other." [96] If the nation adopts the attitude that we are all responsible for each other, Powell feels that great strides could be made.

In December 1991 Democratic congressman Ron Dellums told Powell that he was both the Democratic Party's best hope and worst nightmare—depending on which party he selected. During a 1993 party in Powell's home, Republican consultant David Welch and Democratic commerce secretary Ron Brown each claimed that Powell belonged in his party.

Powell had a wealth of reasons to remain out of the political arena. The wheeling and dealing of Washington disturbed his sense of fair play. He also detested the way people's reputations were scrutinized by the press. As a candidate he would have to speak out on divisive issues such as abortion, on which he normally could remain silent. Once he aired his views, he would lose some support.

What mainly bothered Powell and his wife about running for office was the invasion of privacy faced by public servants. Alma Powell compared it to living in a fishbowl and stated that her choice was to "be out of public life as much as possible." [97]

*With his wife's support, Powell announces in November 1995 that he will not run for president.*

After many years in the public spotlight, the tranquility offered by a happy retirement proved enticing.

In November 1995 Powell announced that he would not run for president. At the same time he declared that he had registered as a Republican, and that it was possible that he would consider a campaign at some future date. He believed that he had fifteen years left in public service, and for the time being he would focus on work benefiting youth. "To be a successful politician, however, requires a calling that I do not yet hear. I believe that I can serve my country in other ways, through charities, educational work, or appointive posts."[98]

However he decides to spend his future years, Powell has already made a significant impact on American society. He has shown to young and old alike that with hard work and determination, one can succeed regardless of color.

*Powell's life is proof that success can be attained through hard work and determination.*

Powell fondly recalls his years in uniform:

In the years I had worn it [a uniform], I had benefited beyond my wildest hopes from all that is good in this country, and I had overcome its lingering faults. I had found something to do with my life that was honorable and useful, that I could do well, and that I loved doing. That is a rare good fortune in anyone's life. My only regret was that I could not do it all over again.[99]

# Notes

------------------------------------------------

## Introduction: "Dreaming About It Isn't Enough"

1. Colin L. Powell, *My American Journey.* New York: Random House, 1995, p. 533.
2. Powell, *My American Journey*, p. 533.
3. Quoted in Howard Means, *Colin Powell.* New York: Donald I. Fine, 1992, p. 35.
4. Powell, *My American Journey*, p. 533.

## Chapter 1: "A Neat Place to Grow Up"

5. Quoted in Steven V. Roberts, "An American Tale: Colin Powell Is Only One Chapter in a Remarkable Immigrant Story," *U.S. News & World Report*, August 21, 1995, p. 5.
6. Powell, *My American Journey*, p. 16.
7. Powell, *My American Journey*, p. 9.
8. Quoted in Steven V. Roberts, "What Next, General Powell?" *U.S. News & World Report*, March 18, 1991, p. 7.
9. Quoted in David Roth, *Sacred Honor: A Biography of Colin Powell.* San Francisco: HarperCollins, 1993, p. 27.
10. Quoted in Academy of Achievement, "The Hall of Public Service: General Colin L. Powell," interview, May 23, 1998. www.achievement.org/autodoc/page/pow0int-1.
11 Powell, *My American Journey*, p. 13.
12. Powell, *My American Journey*, p. 18.
13. Quoted in Roth, *Sacred Honor*, p. 32.
14. Quoted in Roth, *Sacred Honor*, p. 37.
15. Powell, *My American Journey*, p. 29.

## Chapter 2: "A Sense of Belonging"

16. Powell, *My American Journey*, p. 26.

17. Powell, *My American Journey*, p. 28.
18. Powell, *My American Journey*, p. 36.
19. Quoted in Powell, *My American Journey*, p. 34.
20. Quoted in Roth, *Sacred Honor*, p. 42.
21. Quoted in Means, *Colin Powell*, p. 109.
22 Powell, *My American Journey*, p. 39.
23. Powell, *My American Journey*, p. 43.
24. Powell, *My American Journey*, p. 50.
25. Powell, *My American Journey*, p. 62.
26. Powell, *My American Journey*, p. 64.
27. Quoted in Roth, *Sacred Honor*, p. 50.
28. Quoted in Roth, *Sacred Honor*, p. 50.
29. Quoted in Roth, *Sacred Honor*, pp. 54–55.
30. Quoted in Roth, *Sacred Honor*, p. 55.

## Chapter 3: "Half-Hearted Warfare"

31. Powell, *My American Journey*, p. 74.
32. Powell, *My American Journey*, p. 80.
33. Powell, *My American Journey*, p. 82.
34. Powell, *My American Journey*, p. 85.
35. Quoted in Roth, *Sacred Honor*, pp. 68–69.
36. Powell, *My American Journey*, p. 103.
37. Quoted in Andrew Rosenthal, "A General Who Is Right for His Time," *New York Times Biographical Service*, August 1989, p. 763.
38. Powell, *My American Journey*, p. 109.
39. Quoted in Roth, *Sacred Honor*, p. 74.
40. Quoted in Means, *Colin Powell*, p. 12.
41. Quoted in Roth, *Sacred Honor*, pp. 73–74.
42. Quoted in Roth, *Sacred Honor*, p. 83.
43. Powell, *My American Journey*, p. 138.
44. Powell, *My American Journey*, p. 149.

## Chapter 4: "Excellence Is . . . A Prevailing Attitude"

45. Quoted in Powell, *My American Journey*, p. 157.
46. Quoted in Roth, *Sacred Honor*, p. 96.
47. Quoted in Roth, *Sacred Honor*, p. 99.
48. Powell, *My American Journey*, p. 191.
49. Powell, *My American Journey*, p. 198.
50. Quoted in Powell, *My American Journey*, p. 185.
51. Quoted in Roth, *Sacred Honor*, p. 100.

52. Quoted in Means, *Colin Powell*, p. 189.

53. Quoted in Roth, *Sacred Honor*, p. 103.

54. Quoted in Means, *Colin Powell*, p. 192.

55. Powell, *My American Journey*, p. 264.

56. Quoted in Powell, *My American Journey*, p. 273.

57. Quoted in Roth, *Sacred Honor*, p. 107.

58. Quoted in Powell, *My American Journey*, p. 217.

59. Quoted in Roth, *Sacred Honor*, p. 106.

60. Powell, *My American Journey*, p. 218.

## Chapter 5: "A Rare and Valuable Asset"

61. Quoted in Simeon Booker, "Black General at the Summit of U.S. Power," *Ebony*, July 1988, p. 146.

62. Powell, *My American Journey*, p. 301.

63. Quoted in Andrew Rosenthal, "Military Chief: Man of Action and of Politics," *New York Times Biographical Service*, August 1990, p. 749.

64. Powell, *My American Journey*, p. 323.

65. Quoted in Roth, *Sacred Honor*, p. 120.

66. Quoted in Judith Graham, ed., *1988 Current Biography Yearbook*. New York: H. W. Wilson, 1988, p. 457.

67. Quoted in Roth, *Sacred Honor*, p. 122.

68. Quoted in Booker, "Black General at the Summit of U.S. Power," p. 146.

69. Quoted in Roth, *Sacred Honor*, p. 127.

70. Quoted in Carl T. Rowan, "Called to Service: The Colin Powell Story," *Reader's Digest*, December 1989, p. 126.

71. Quoted in Booker, "Black General at the Summit of U.S. Power," p. 137.

72. Quoted in Barrett Seaman, "A 'Complete Soldier' Makes It," *Time*, August 21, 1989, p. 24.

## Chapter 6: "Go in Big, and End It Quickly"

73. Powell, *My American Journey*, p. 427.

74. Quoted in Roberts, "What Next, General Powell?" p. 6.

75. Quoted in Rosenthal, "Military Chief," p. 748.

76. Quoted in Michael R. Gordon and Bernard E. Trainor, *The Generals' War: The Inside Story of the Conflict in the Gulf*. Boston: Little, Brown, 1995, p. 33.

77. Powell, *My American Journey*, p. 490.

78. Quoted in Rosenthal, "Military Chief," pp. 748–49.
79. Powell, *My American Journey*, p. 487.
80. Powell, *My American Journey*, p. 513.
81. Quoted in Academy of Achievement, "The Hall of Public Service."
82. Quoted in Brian Duffy, "The Right Stuff," *U.S. News & World Report*, February 4, 1991, pp. 1–2.
83. Quoted in Gordon and Trainor, *The Generals' War*, p. xv.
84. Quoted in Roth, *Sacred Honor*, p. 207.
85. Quoted in Powell, *My American Journey*, p. 535.
86. Powell, *My American Journey*, p. 532.

## Chapter 7: "You Did Well by America"

87. Powell, *My American Journey*, p. 574.
88. Quoted in Roberts, "What Next, General Powell?" pp. 8–9.
89. Quoted in Roth, *Sacred Honor*, pp. 152–53.
90. Quoted in Roth, *Sacred Honor*, p. 185.
91. Quoted in Steven V. Roberts, Bruce B. Auster, and Michael Barone, "Colin Powell, Superstar: Will America's Top General Trade His Uniform for a Future in Politics?" *U.S. News & World Report*, September 20, 1993, p. 14.
92. Quoted in Powell, *My American Journey*, p. 590.
93. Powell, *My American Journey*, p. 592.
94. Quoted in Academy of Achievement, "The Hall of Public Service."
95. Powell, *My American Journey*, p. 554.
96. Quoted in Powell, *My American Journey*, p. 611.
97. Quoted in Roberts, Auster, and Barone, "Colin Powell, Superstar," pp. 17–18.
98. Powell, *My American Journey*, p. 609.
99. Powell, *My American Journey*, p. 591.

# Important Dates in the Life of Colin Powell

**1937**
Colin Luther Powell is born in New York City on April 5.

**1954**
Powell graduates from Morris High School; enrolls in the City College of New York (CCNY); enters the campus Reserve Officers' Training Corps (ROTC).

**1958**
Powell graduates from CCNY; finishes at the top of his ROTC class; is commissioned a second lieutenant in the army; attends Infantry Officer Basic Course; attends ranger and airborne schools.

**1959**
Powell commands a platoon stationed at the Fulda Gap along West Germany's border; is promoted to first lieutenant.

**1961**
Powell commands a company of soldiers at Fort Devens; meets Alma Johnson on a blind date.

**1962**
Powell marries Alma Johnson; is promoted to captain; arrives in Vietnam for his first tour.

**1963**
Son Michael is born; racial unrest erupts in the United States; Powell is injured in Vietnam.

**1965**
Daughter Linda is born; Powell is promoted to major.

**1967**
Powell attends the Command and General Staff College at Fort Leavenworth.

**1968**
Powell returns to Vietnam for his second tour; though injured, rescues three people in a helicopter crash.

**1970**
Daughter Annemarie is born; Powell is promoted to lieutenant colonel.

**1971**
Powell earns a master's degree in business administration from George Washington University.

**1972**
Powell is named a White House fellow and works for the Office of Management and Budget.

**1973**
Powell receives command of the First Battalion, Thirty-second Infantry in South Korea.

**1975**
Powell studies at the National War College.

**1976**
Powell receives command of the Second Brigade, 101st Airborne Division; is promoted to colonel.

**1977**
Powell serves as an assistant to John Kester in the Defense Department.

**1978**
Powell is promoted to brigadier general; serves as assistant to Charles Duncan in the Energy Department.

**1981**
Powell serves as assistant commander of the Fourth Mechanized Infantry Division.

**1982**
Powell serves as deputy commander of Combined Arms Combat Development at Fort Leavenworth; becomes top military assistant to the secretary of defense.

## 1983

Powell is promoted to major general; helps coordinate the invasion of Grenada.

## 1986

Powell helps plan an air attack on Libya; receives command of the V Corps in West Germany; is promoted to lieutenant general.

## 1987

Powell becomes deputy national security adviser; then becomes national security adviser; son Michael is injured in Germany.

## 1989

Powell is promoted to four-star general; receives command of the Forces Command; becomes chairman of the Joint Chiefs of Staff; conducts an invasion of Panama to oust Manuel Noriega.

## 1990

Iraqi troops invade Kuwait; American forces begin arriving in Saudi Arabia.

## 1991

Powell directs Operation Desert Storm; is named for a second term as chairman of the Joint Chiefs of Staff.

## 1993

Powell retires from the army; is knighted by the queen of England; is courted by both major political parties as a presidential candidate.

## 1995

Powell announces he will not run as a presidential candidate.

# For Further Reading

Roger Barr, *The Vietnam War*. San Diego: Lucent Books, 1991. A good summary of the war for junior high school students.

Martin Binkin and Mark J. Eitelberg, *Blacks in the Military*. Washington, DC: Brookings Institution, 1982. A serious study of African Americans in the armed forces.

Rose Blue and Corinne J. Naden, *Colin Powell: Straight to the Top*. Brookfield, CT: Millbrook, 1991. A biography of Powell written for upper elementary students.

Warren Brown, *Colin Powell*. New York: Chelsea House, 1992. A biography intended for the junior high school market that includes basic information on Powell.

Robert Cwiklik, *Bill Clinton*. Brookfield, CT: Millbrook, 1991. A brief biography of the president targeted for the elementary level.

Jim Haskins, *Colin Powell*. New York: Scholastic, 1992. A useful short biography of Powell that appeared shortly after the war with Iraq; written for the junior high school market.

Frank B. Latham, *The Rise and Fall of "Jim Crow," 1865–1964*. New York: Franklin Watts, 1969. A good short summary of segregation in the South and efforts to change it.

John Narzo, *The Persian Gulf War*. San Diego: Lucent Books, 1991. A superb summary of the war for junior high school students that is very helpful in understanding the events leading to the fighting.

Dorothy Sterling, *Tear Down the Walls!* Garden City, NY: Doubleday, 1968. A well-written summary of the civil rights movement intended for the junior high school market.

# Works Consulted
-------------------------------------------

## Books

Taylor Branch, *Parting the Waters: America in the King Years, 1954–1963*. New York: Simon & Schuster, 1988. An outstanding portrait of segregation and the civil rights movement that engulfed the United States immediately preceding the Vietnam years. This book delivers an essential understanding of the world in which Colin Powell grew up and in which he was educated.

*Certain Victory: The U.S. Army in the Gulf War.* Washington, DC: Office of the Chief of Staff, United States Army, 1993. An official history of the army in Desert Storm.

John Hope Franklin, *From Slavery to Freedom.* New York: Knopf, 1974. A general history of African Americans in the United States, written by one of the foremost historians of our day.

Richard Goldstein, *Mine Eyes Have Seen: A First-Person History of Events That Shaped America.* New York: Simon & Schuster, 1997. A general history of the United States that contains personal accounts of the civil rights movement and Vietnam.

Michael R. Gordon and Bernard E. Trainor, *The Generals' War: The Inside Story of the Conflict in the Gulf.* Boston: Little, Brown, 1995. A sometimes harsh examination of the military moves of Powell, Schwarzkopf, and other top commanders in the Gulf War. The book is helpful for understanding the military thinking that guided the war.

Judith Graham, ed., *1988 Current Biography Yearbook.* New York: H. W. Wilson, 1988. A collection of biographies of influential people, including a concise summary of Powell's career.

Howard Means, *Colin Powell.* New York: Donald I. Fine, 1992. Journalist Howard Means interviewed numerous people for this biography of Colin Powell. While much useful information is included, the writing is not the smoothest.

Linda R. Monk, ed., *Ordinary Americans: U.S. History Through the Eyes of Everyday People.* New York: Close Up, 1994. A survey of American history based on personal accounts by people involved in important events, including civil rights, Vietnam, and the Gulf War.

M. E. Morris, *Norman Schwarzkopf: Road to Triumph.* New York: St. Martin's, 1991. A decent biography of the Gulf War general written for the adult market.

Bernard C. Nalty, *Strength for the Fight: A History of Black Americans in the Military.* New York: Free, 1986. Though the book was written before the Gulf War, it provides helpful information on African American efforts to serve in the military.

Colin L. Powell, *My American Journey.* New York: Random House, 1995. This autobiography is the essential source for information on Powell. Easy to read, the book is filled with excellent material, stories about the man, and lessons from his life.

David Roth, *Sacred Honor: A Biography of Colin Powell.* San Francisco: HarperCollins, 1993. Written by a former Powell aide, this book contains some illuminating information, especially about Powell's personal life. However, the book suffers from poor writing and editing.

H. Norman Schwarzkopf, *It Doesn't Take a Hero.* New York: Bantam Books, 1992. This memoir delivers powerful material on his role in the Gulf War and includes relevant comments on Powell.

Bob Woodward, *The Commanders.* New York : Simon & Schuster, 1991. Written by one of the most respected reporters in Washington, this book is a hard-hitting examination of how Powell and Schwarzkopf operated the war.

## Periodicals

Bruce B. Auster, "In the Footsteps of Two Georges," *U.S. News & World Report,* February 4, 1991.

Simeon Booker, "Black General at the Summit of U.S. Power," *Ebony*, July 1988.

Brian Duffy, "The Right Stuff," *U.S. News & World Report*, February 4, 1991.

Laurie Harris, "Colin Powell," *Biography Today*, 1992 Annual Cumulation.

Steven V. Roberts, "An American Tale: Colin Powell Is Only One Chapter in a Remarkable Immigrant Story," *U.S. News & World Report*, August 21, 1995.

————, "What Next, General Powell?" *U.S. News & World Report*, March 18, 1991.

Steven V. Roberts, Bruce B. Auster, and Michael Barone, "Colin Powell, Superstar: Will America's Top General Trade His Uniform for a Future in Politics?" *U.S. News & World Report*, September 20, 1993.

Andrew Rosenthal, "A General Who Is Right for His Time," *New York Times Biographical Service*, August 1989.

————, "Military Chief: Man of Action and of Politics," *New York Times Biographical Service*, August 1990.

Carl T. Rowan, "Called to Service: The Colin Powell Story," *Reader's Digest*, December 1989.

Barrett Seaman, "A 'Complete Soldier' Makes It," *Time*, August 21, 1989.

John F. Stacks, "The Powell Factor," *Time*, July 10, 1995.

John Walcott, "The Man to Watch," *U.S. News & World Report*, August 21, 1995.

Mortimer B. Zuckerman, "Behind the Powell Phenomenon," *U.S. News & World Report*, August 21, 1995.

## Internet Resources

Academy of Achievement, "The Hall of Public Service: General Colin L. Powell," interview, May 23, 1998. www.achievement. org/autodoc/page/pow0int-1.

# Index

------------------------------------------------

# Picture Credits

# About the Author

John F. Wukovits is a junior high school teacher and writer from Trenton, Michigan, who specializes in history and biography. Besides biographies of Anne Frank, Jim Carrey, Stephen King, and Martin Luther King Jr. for Lucent, he has written biographies of Barry Sanders, Tim Allen, Jack Nicklaus, Vince Lombardi, Wyatt Earp, and World War II commander Clifton Sprague. A graduate of the University of Notre Dame, Wukovits is the father of three daughters—Amy, Julie, and Karen.